Isob⌐⌐ ·
G⌐
BRY⌐
Ad⌐

CW00495852

0 0 4 5 9 7

ENGLISH FACULTY
LIBRARY

THE GEORGIAN POETS

LASCELLES ABERCROMBIE
a photograph taken in 1919
by courtesy of the owner, J. Cooper

RUPERT BROOKE
a photograph by Sherrill Schell, 1913
by courtesy of the National Portrait Gallery, London

JOHN DRINKWATER
a portrait by E. H. Kennington, 1917
by courtesy of Samuel French Ltd

WILFRID WILSON GIBSON
a photograph by Sherrill Schell
by courtesy of the National Portrait Gallery, London

THE GEORGIAN POETS

THE GEORGIAN POETS
Abercrombie, Brooke, Drinkwater, Gibson and Thomas

RENNIE PARKER

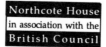

Northcote House
in association with the
British Council

© Copyright 1999 by Rennie Parker

First published in 1999 by Northcote House Publishers Ltd, Plymbridge House, Estover Road, Plymouth PL6 7PY, United Kingdom.
Tel: +44 (01752) 202368 Fax: +44 (01752) 202330.

All rights reserved. No part of this work may be reproduced or stored in an information retrieval system (other than short extracts for the purposes of review) without the express permission of the Publishers given in writing.

British Library Cataloguing-in-Publication Data
A catalogue record for this book is available from the British Library

ISBN 0-7463-0899-X

Typeset by PDQ Typesetting, Newcastle-under-Lyme
Printed and bound in the United Kingdom

Contents

Acknowledgements

Acknowledgement is due to the following people and organizations for their generous help and assistance over textual and copyright matters: Mr J. Cooper for Lascelles Abercrombie; King's College Library (Modern Archives) for Rupert Brooke; Mr L. Toynbee for Rosalind Murray; Samuel French Ltd and Mrs Drinkwater Self for John Drinkwater; Macmillan General Books for permission to quote from the *Collected Poems* by Wilfrid Wilson Gibson; Mrs Myfanwy Thomas for Edward Thomas. Thanks too, for the helpful suggestions from Caroline Bowd, Richard Emeny and Linda Hart, and to the staff of Cheltenham & Gloucester College of Higher Education, Birmingham University Heslop Room, the Bodleian Library, Oxford, and Leeds University Brotherton Library.

Biographical Outlines

LASCELLES ABERCROMBIE (1881–1938)

1881	9 January: born at Ashton upon Mersey, near Manchester, penultimate child in a family of eleven (two died in childhood), to Sarah Anne and William Abercrombie, a stockbroker.
1889	Family moves to Brooklands, near Manchester. Early interest in natural history.
1895–1900	At Malvern College. Good academic record, becoming Head of House, School Prefect, and Prefect of Choir. Writing poetry, but considers science as his career.
1897	Wins Old Malvernian Science Prize, worth £5.
1900	Begins studying chemistry at Manchester University. Contributes to *The Trawl*, a journal organized by university friends and his brother Patrick.
1902	Leaves university without taking a degree. Moves to Birkenhead and lives with friends. Works as a quantity surveyor in Liverpool.
1906	March: meets Catherine Gwatkin, artist and designer, founder of the Sandon Studios Society in Liverpool.
1907	March: first publication, 'Blind', in the *Independent Review*. Begins unpaid newspaper work. October: gives up quantity surveying to concentrate on poetry; devises his first collection. Financially supported by his older sister Ursula, and by Mrs Leila Reynolds, who had wealth from the cotton industry.
1908	January: *Interludes and Poems* published. August: journalist on the *Liverpool Courier*.

1909	January: marries Catherine Gwatkin. Plans to live in the country, but is living in Birkenhead.
1910	Searches for freelance work in London; meets Yeats, Laurence Binyon and Masefield. Abercrombies move to Much Marcle, Herefordshire.
	September: *Mary and the Bramble* published by the author.
1911	April: Abercrombies move to The Gallows, Ryton, Dymock. First act of *The Sale of St Thomas* published by the author. Visits Italy in October.
1912	*Deborah* (a three-act play) published; *Emblems of Love* (poems) and *Thomas Hardy: A Critical Study* published.
1913	*Speculative Dialogues* published. Reviews regularly for the *Nation*, the *Manchester Guardian*, and the *Daily News* between 1911 and 1914. Visits Italy.
1914	*The End of the World*; Catherine Abercrombie designs the format for *New Numbers*.
1916	War work in a munitions factory in Liverpool.
1919	Brief return to Dymock, where most of *Twelve Idyls and Other Poems* is written.
1919–22	Lecturer in Poetry at Liverpool University.
1922–9	Professor of English, Leeds University.
1924	Lectures at Bangor (University of Wales) and Cambridge on 'The Idea of Great Poetry'.
1925–7	*The Idea of Great Poetry* (Martin Secker) published. Broadcasts for the BBC on poetry; lectures at the Sorbonne and Strasbourg. Becomes ill with diabetes.
1928	*Twelve Idyls* published.
1929–36	Professor of English at Bedford College, London.
1930	Joins the BBC Advisory Committee on Spoken English. Honorary DLitt conferred by Cambridge University. *The Poems of Lascelles Abercrombie* published.
1931	April: British representative at Skyros for the unveiling of the Rupert Brooke memorial.
1932	*Principles of Literary Criticism* (Gollancz) published.
1935	Introduces Dylan Thomas to Richard Church, editor at Dent's, Thomas's subsequent publisher. Gives lectures on Wordsworth at Johns Hopkins University, Baltimore.

1936	January: Goldsmith's Reader in English and Fellow of Merton College, Oxford.
1937	Elected as a Fellow of the Royal Academy.
1938	October: dies of a gastric haemorrhage and diabetes.

WILFRID WILSON GIBSON (1878–1962)

1878	2 October: born at Battle Hill Terrace, Hexham, Northumberland, into a large family. Father, William Pattison Gibson, is the town chemist. Educated at home by his half-sister Elizabeth; decides to work as a writer from the outset, following her example.
1902	*The Golden Helm* published: 'medieval' romantic poetry.
1904	*Urlyn the Harper* published.
1907	Short period of social work in the slums of Glasgow. *The Stonefolds* and *On the Threshold* published; an abrupt change of style compared to his previous works.
1910	*Daily Bread* published. Friendship with Drinkwater begins.
1912	Leaves Hexham for London; meets Monro and Brooke. *Fires* published, widely praised.
1913	*Womenkind* published; performed on stage as a music-hall item. Lives at the Poetry Bookshop. Marries Geraldine Audrey Townshend, Monro's assistant. Moves to the Old Nailshop, Greenway, near Dymock.
1914	Assists the Abercrombies with *New Numbers*; 'Bloody Bush Edge' published.
1915	*Battle* published.
1916	October: starts on a reading tour of the United States. Family relocated to West Malvern, Worcestershire.
1917	*Collected Poems* published in America. Finally accepted for military service in England.
1918–25	Reading tours around Britain; leads a busy life as a writer in demand.
1922	*Krindlesyke* published.
1924	*Kestrel Edge and Other Plays* published.
1925	*Collected Poems* published by Macmillan.
1926	Lives in Letchworth, Hertfordshire.

1933–6	Lives at Nassington Road, London NW3.
1938	*Coming and Going* published. Living at Golder's Green, London.
1939	Eldest daughter, Audrey, killed in a landslide in the Alps. The Gibsons move to East Hendred, near Wantage, Oxford. Gibson under suspicion due to his German son-in-law.
1941	*The Alert* published.
1942	*Challenge* (OUP) published.
1947	*Coldknuckles* (Frederick Muller) published.
1950	Living at West Byfleet, Surrey. *Within Four Walls* published. Geraldine dies. Gibson publishes no more poetry.
1962	26 May: dies in a nursing home at Virginia Water, Surrey.

EDWARD THOMAS (1878–1917)

1878	3 March: Philip Edward Thomas born in Lambeth, London, eldest in a family of sons, to Mary Elizabeth and Philip Henry Thomas, a civil servant.
1883–94	At school, concluding with Battersea Grammar and St Paul's, London.
1895	Friendship with Helen Noble as a result of visiting James Ashcroft Noble. Begins career as essayist.
1897	*The Woodland Life* published.
1898	Scholarship to Lincoln College, Oxford.
1899	Marries Helen Noble at Fulham Registry Office.
1900	Second-class degree in History. Decides on full-time writing career. Lives in poverty in London.
1901	Moves to Rose Acre Cottage, Bearsted, Kent.
1902	Regular reviewer for the *Daily Chronicle*.
1903	First commission, *Oxford*, published.
1904–6	Lives near Sevenoaks, Kent.
1904–10	Commissions and reviews, including *Richard Jefferies* (pub. 1909). Researches, writes, and seeks subsequent work.
1908	Brief period working for the Royal Commission for Welsh Monuments.

1911	Works on seven books, including *George Borrow* (pub. 1912).
1912	Writes for Harold Monro's *Poetry Review*, the *English Review*, and the *Nation*. Meets Eleanor Farjeon, writer and children's author.
1913	Moves to Steep village, Hampshire. Meets Robert Frost in London. Novel, *The Happy-Go-Lucky Morgans*, published.
1914	*In Pursuit of Spring* published. Visits Frost, and spends August in Ledington, associating with Frost and the resident 'Dymock Poets'. Begins writing poetry, November/December.
1915	Ankle injury confines him to Steep, writing poetry. Decides to enlist rather than join Frost. *The Life of the Duke of Marlborough* prepared. Enlists in the Artist's Rifles; billeted to Hare Hall Camp, Essex. Poems begin to be accepted under pseudonym 'Edward Eastaway'.
1916	Awarded £300 instead of a Civil List pension. Applies for a commission in the Royal Artillery. Selection of verse considered by Selwyn & Blount.
1917	January: stationed near Arras. Eighteen poems published in *An Annual of New Poetry*. 9 April: Killed by shell-blast during the first hour of the Battle of Arras. *Poems* published by Selwyn & Blount.
1918	*Last Poems* (Selwyn & Blount).

JOHN DRINKWATER (1882–1937)

1882	1 June: born in Leytonstone, Essex (now in Greater London), the son of Albert Edwin Drinkwater, a schoolmaster and actor, and Annie Beck, his first wife. Develops a love of the countryside when young.
1897–1901	Leaves Oxford High School and begins his career in the insurance industry at Nottingham, aged 15.
1902–7	Relocated to Birmingham; progresses as an insurance officer while starting his work as a poet. Begins his involvement with *The Pilgrim Players* (initially an amateur society) and the impresario Barry Jackson.

1908	*Lyrical and Other Poems* published by Harold Monro's early Samurai Press.
1911	Marries Kathleen Walpole (a Pilgrim Player) in Cheetham, Lancashire. *Poems of Men and Hours* (David Nutt) published. Becomes President of the Birmingham Dramatic and Literary Club; meets many writers as a result. Begins to visit Abercrombie.
1912	Contributes to *Rhythm* (*The Blue Review*) and *Poetry Review*; present at a planning meeting for *Georgian Poetry*. *Poems of Love and Earth* published.
1913	The opening season of Birmingham Repertory Theatre, where he is installed as General Manager, with frequent appearances as Producer and cast member (pseud. John Darnley). Included in the plans for *New Numbers*.
1914	*Poems 1908–1914* and *Rebellion* published.
1914–15	Works on the Georgian drama productions at Birmingham, including *The End of the World*, and *King Lear's Wife*.
1915	*Swords and Ploughshares* published: one of his best collections. Living at Balsall Heath, Birmingham.
1916	*Olton Pools* published.
1917	*Tides, Prose Papers*, and *Pawns: Three Poetic Plays* published. Moves to Far Oakridge, near Stroud, Gloucestershire.
1918	*Abraham Lincoln* performed and published; Drinkwater now an established playwright.
1919	*Loyalties* published.
1921	Separated from Kathleen Walpole; meets Daisy Kennedy, a violinist.
1923	*Collected Poems* published by Sidgwick & Jackson.
1924	Marries Daisy Kennedy.
1925	*Collected Plays* published.
1921–37	Prolific output as a playwright, including *Mary Stuart and Robert E. Lee*; equally prolific as a poet. Meets many famous writers, including Wells, Bennett, Shaw and Galsworthy. Also knows James Joyce and the poet/librettist Hugo von Hofmannsthal. Visits the USA in connection with his plays.
1927–8	Lives in London at Evelyn Gardens, SW7.
1928	*Charles James Fox*, a historical study, published.

1929	Lives at Pepys House, Brampton, near Huntingdon.
1930	Lives in London again, Highgate Village.
1937	25 March: dies at the age of 55, reputedly from overwork.

RUPERT BROOKE (1887–1915)

1887	3 August: Rupert Chawner Brooke born in Rugby, Warwickshire, the second son of Mary Ruth and William Parker Brooke, housemaster at Rugby school.
1901	Enters Rugby school, after attending a preparatory school at Hillbrow, nearby.
1903	Writing poetry seriously; earliest publishable works date from this period.
1906–9	A high-profile career at King's College, Cambridge, writing and acting. Associates with artists, writers and intellectuals, including the Stracheys, Keynes, Raverats and Darwins.
1909	Obtains a second-class degree in Classics. Moves to Grantchester, living at The Orchard. President of the University Fabian Society. Returns to Rugby after his father's death, working as a housemaster for two months. Begins a complicated liaison with Noel Olivier and subsequently Katherine (Ka) Cox.
1911	*Poems* published. Associating with Edward Marsh.
1912	Increasing frustration in his private life causes a breakdown. Travels to Germany; writes 'The Old Vicarage Grantchester', while in Berlin. Writes *Lithuania*.
	September: devises the plan of 'Georgian poetry' with Marsh.
1913	Obtains a Fellowship at King's College. Visits America and Canada; travel reports published in the *Westminster Gazette*.
1913–14	Travels to the South Seas; writing poetry.
1914	June: returns to England.
	September: joins the Royal Naval Division after the outbreak of war. October: stationed at Antwerp.
1914–15	Writes the 'war sonnets'; publication in *New Numbers*.

1915   23 April: dies of septicaemia as a result of an insect
          bite while on his way to the Dardanelles. Buried on
          the Greek island of Skyros.
          June: *Poems* 1914 published; a great popular success.
          Other Brooke writings receive posthumous publica-
          tion, including *Letters from America* (Sidgwick &
          Jackson, 1923) and *Democracy and the Arts* (Hart-
          Davis, 1946).

Abbreviations

P	*Collected Poems 1905–1925* by Wilfrid Gibson (Macmillan, 1926)
PET	*The Collected Poems of Edward Thomas*, ed. R. George Thomas (Oxford University Press, 1978)
P	*The Dymock Poets* by Sean Street (Bridgend: Seren Borderlines, 1994)
PA	*Once They Lived In Gloucestershire: A Dymock Poets' Anthology*, ed. Linda Hart (Lechlade: Green Branch Press, 1995)
M	*Edward Marsh, Patron of the Arts: A Biography* by Christopher Hassall
R	*The Georgian Revolt: Rise and Fall of a Poetic Ideal, 1910–22* by Robert H. Ross (Faber & Faber, 1967)
	Interludes and Poems by Lascelles Abercrombie (John Lane/ The Bodley Head, 1928)
LA	*The Poems of Lascelles Abercrombie* (Oxford University Press, 1930)
WRB	*The Poetical Works of Rupert Brooke*, ed. Geoffrey Keynes (Faber & Faber, 1946)
B	*Rupert Brooke: A Biography* by Christopher Hassall (Faber & Faber, 1964)

Introduction

The 'Georgian' poets, the 'Muse Colony', the 'Dymock Poets'...
all these terms have been used to describe the pre-First World
War writers who were associated for a time with a specific
geographical area, slightly south of Ledbury on the Gloucester-
shire/Herefordshire border. Detailed accounts of these writers
and their Dymock milieu were published in 1992 (Keith Clark's
The Muse Colony) and 1994 (Sean Street's *The Dymock Poets*), so
this study does not set out to repeat the material already
available, or to compete with the narrative and literary historical
emphasis found in these well-researched and readable books.
The intention of this introductory study is to uncover more
about the poetry itself, and to bring forward the themes and
undercurrents found in the poetry being written around the
Georgian years. This will not only help to right the balance in
favour of the poetry itself, since some of it is unjustly neglected;
but it will also support traditional literary historical studies as
they exist at the moment.

The term 'Georgian poet' has latterly come to represent a
writer of debilitated ruralist verse, and some of the less happy
products of our sample group (particularly Drinkwater) might
conform to this description. At the time, 'Georgian' meant
something else entirely, and was seen as a reaction against the
ornate late-Victorian style in poetry, with the term itself being
deliberately invented by the influential Edward Marsh[1] as a
kind of marketing strategy. The movement, once it was under
way and the subject of promotion by anthologies and journals,
succumbed to its unfortunate timing near the outbreak of World
War I, and the relentless criticism of vigorous anti-Georgians
such as Ezra Pound, Middleton Murry and Richard Aldington.

Furthermore, 'Georgian' poetry, when seen in its 1914

context, tends to be defined by what it is not. It is not Imagist, it is not wholly about war, and it is consequently harder to theorize about in comparison with the boundaries drawn by other 'isms' of the same period. As if to add to the difficulty of defining Georgianism, it is unlikely that many of the poets concerned ever thought of themselves as members of a Georgian stable. In fact, they may have felt obstructed by such a title, with its paradoxical associations of tradition and monarchy. Marsh was an asset to the poets examined here, but he was also a diplomat and a player on the world stage; 'Georgian' it was, whether the poets wanted it or not. Here is Rupert Brooke on the matter in 1914:

> it's generally agreed that Marsh has got Georgianism on the brain, and will shortly issue a series of Georgian poker-work: and establish a band of Georgian cooks.[2]

What survives down to us as a brave attempt at marketing new English poetry had begun life as little more than a literary joke, one thought up by Brooke himself, then seized on and developed by Marsh. The full story is provided by Christopher Hassall in *Edward Marsh: A Biography*. Georgianism collided into existence through accident, and so did the Dymock group; and the poets who associated for a time at Dymock were a microcosm of all that was good and bad about the movement in its wider sense.

The Georgian/Dymock Poet circle, for the purposes of this study, is restricted to those who were most regularly associated with Edward Marsh, with each other as colleagues and correspondents, and with other relevant publications such as *New Numbers* in 1914. This helps to establish a coherent 'Georgian' grouping without falling into the trap which Edward Marsh himself fell into – that of yoking together too many diverse writers for the purposes of his scheme. But in reality, this small sample group, united by friendship ties and by geographical proximity, was neither exclusive nor particularly countrified. Only the brief American visitor Robert Frost was a farmer in any real way, and all of the poets depended on literary contacts for reviewing work and financial help. Brooke, for all his pretensions at 'neo-pagan' life and his camping expeditions with fashionable people, was a University man *par excellence*, far

2

removed from the rural poverty as seen and written about by his friend Wilfrid Gibson. Some readers may be surprised at the inclusion of Edward Thomas and Robert Frost here, yet Frost achieved his breakthrough as an important poet at the hands of a Georgian publisher,[3] and was close to the original ideal of vigorous communication and environmental awareness. Thomas, too, was regarded as a 'Georgian' by his contemporaries, who were prepared to forego publication in Marsh's anthologies so that he could be established as a poet.[4] The continuation of Georgianism as an undercurrent in English verse is largely due to Thomas's 'language not to be betrayed'.

There may not have been a deliberate colony, but the Dymock group were undoubtedly friends. It was due to Abercrombie's presence at Ryton[5] that Gibson and Frost moved into the area, while Thomas moved into Oldfields[6] to be near Frost. Brooke was drawn to Gibson by friendship, and the unassuming Northumbrian let the golden boy of Cambridge – a huge success before his death as well as after – use his upstairs room at the Old Nailshop, Greenway.[7] However, like any circle associated by professional ties as well as friendship, rivalry surfaced from time to time. Some of this is recounted by Street and Clark, and it would be foolish to suppose that competitiveness and posturing played no part. Drinkwater may have been suspected of the latter by Catherine Abercrombie, who described:

> how he read some of his poems to us straight away, and how I wished he would not, as he turned himself into a fashionable parson, voice and all, and eyes to the ceiling, to do it. (DP 38)

Yet Drinkwater was an actor and playwright as well as a poet, with a successful career at Birmingham Repertory Theatre. His artistic reputation, like Lascelles Abercrombie's, has fared badly.

Feminist literary critics can make little headway with the group, for the women connected with the Georgian/Dymock circle have been all but written out of the story. This is reinforced in the Street account, with its cover picture of Abercrombie and Gibson with Marsh and Drinkwater, reproduced without the women involved. The full picture appears in the text between pages 96 and 97. Yet, in real life, the female contribution was noticeable, for Geraldine Gibson was a Newnham-educated career woman, working at Harold Monro's

Poetry Bookshop before her marriage. Secondary source comments would suggest that Geraldine was a hausfrau, plain and undemanding – yet she had enjoyed an independent life prior to becoming Mrs Gibson, having accomplished feats such as climbing the Matterhorn and tiger-shooting on safari. With her bookkeeping and secretarial skills, she was an ideal partner for keeping standards up and poverty at bay. Catherine Abercrombie, meanwhile, had trained as an artist; she was the practical workhorse behind the *New Numbers* editions in 1914. Along with the generous-minded Helen Thomas and the anarchically undomesticated Elinor Frost, they offered far more than a vague home environment against which the drama of being a male poet was played out. One of the most engaging associated characters is surely Eleanor Farjeon (1881–1965), whose sociability and stout constitution enabled her to 'drink all the poets of Gloucestershire under the table'. Her book *Edward Thomas: The Last Four Years* includes an amusing account of a meeting between four of the Dymock Poets in 1914, and revealing thumbnail portraits of Gibson and Abercrombie. Unfortunately, this study is necessarily confined to the works written by the men, but there is enough background material supplied in the bibliography for future students to explore gender studies in connection with the Dymock legend. Eleanor Farjeon herself achieved enduring popularity as a writer for children, and her verse is often anthologized.

The following chapters occasionally mention J. W. (John Wilton) Haines, who knew most of the Georgian poets who lived in his home county of Gloucestershire. He was a solicitor by profession, but his interests were in poetry and botany, which drew him to explore the countryside much in the same way as the writers. He was related by marriage to the Abercrombies and knew Thomas well; but Thomas was a little irritated by Haines's solidity and regularity, and it is fair to describe Haines's own poetry as being without much vital spark. Nevertheless, he wrote many perceptive comments about the Dymock poets, and acted on their behalf when legal disputes threatened. No study of these poets would be complete without mentioning the encouragement and support he gave to them.

The Georgian poets included here were not, of course, the only writers who fell under that description once the movement had been launched. Some, for example John Masefield (1878–1967), were towering figures whose diversity of poetic output and long careers were not dependent on the Georgian anthologies as a launchpad for their aims as writers – in the case of Abercrombie, Brooke and Drinkwater, the publicity generated by the Georgian movement was a springboard to further activity. The poets included in this study are the 'first-wave' Georgians, in at the beginning and constant in their attachment to all that the short-lived but influential movement symbolized between 1912 and 1922.

1

Lascelles Abercrombie
'What great things I meant to do'

'Anyone who has ever heard him will remember the charm of his reading voice, the best reading voice of any poet known to me, or indeed of any man' (J. W. Haines).[1] This is not the photogenic and charismatic Rupert Brooke, but the little-known poet Lascelles Abercrombie (1881–1938), whose reputation has not survived, despite the enthusiasm shown for his works by critics during his lifetime. Although Abercrombie largely gave up writing poetry during the First World War and turned increasingly to criticism during the 1920s, his reputation as an academic and literary pundit were sufficient to guarantee a high profile until his death; so it is not merely an early cessation of his poetic activity which caused a downturn in his creative reputation after 1938.

Neither is this posthumous lack of profile due to a reluctance in effort from Abercrombie himself while he was alive. Letters and reports agree that he was an engaging person, witty, knowledgeable, and unstuffy. An early talent for natural history and science meant that he was not confined to bookish pursuits, and at least one visitor to The Gallows at Ryton had a first-hand experience of the Abercrombie ingenuity.[2] He debated and wrote letters with relish, and met figures as diverse as Edward Marsh and Aleister Crowley.[3] He was also the subject of a notorious literary tirade from Ezra Pound, who challenged him to a duel; Abercrombie's unruffled reaction was to suggest that he and Pound should attack one another with rolled-up copies of their unsold poems. Clearly, Abercrombie could attract the attention of the famous and the infamous; and the following extract from a postcard provides an example of his cheerful hospitality towards friends:

6

do come soon, as soon as your germs clear off (we have babies). Either come with Marsh, or if that means complex political arrangements hard to come by, then by yourself...As far as we are concerned, there is no need to wait for the next feast of the church. The sooner the better. Many congratulations on the award...[4]

On personality grounds alone, the wide-ranging Abercrombie, with his escape to the country, his bohemian way of life, and his constant literary activity, does not suggest an outcome of spiritual disappointment and temporal failure. Yet this is what he felt towards the end of his life. His poems represented 'unrealised ambition' (*PLA*, p. v) and he had not lived up to his expectations: 'Mine was an ambition that would have harmed no one: it was but to live in the country and write poetry. I was not equal to it' (*DP*, 152–3). His dream did not become a permanent reality, and therefore he had failed.

Twenty years previously he had been a founder member of the Georgian literary movement, with great things expected of him. The following critical reactions show the excitable verdict of several reviewers, not usually known for their generosity towards the Georgians:

> Of all the poetic talents which have appeared since the start of the century his is the most conspicuous union of breadth and intensity. (*Times Literary Supplement*, in *EM* 686)

> ...astonishing power of dramatic psychological analysis. He is a vehement, imaginative thinker. If he were a race-horse he might be described as by Browning out of Elizabethan drama... (*Nation*, 8 March 1913)

> In a swift, molten cascade Mr. Abercrombie pours this amazing amalgam of thought, vision, imagination out of the crucible of his mind, and it packs his verse...['The Olympians'] is an amazing achievement. It breaks down all the neat little wattles of the critics for keeping their poetical flocks in order. (*TLS*, 19 March 1914)

He is perceived as a leader among poets, with an abundant facility of imagination and a tendency to break the mould.

In Gloucestershire, meanwhile, the praise was much the same. Although J. W. Haines was a reliable friend to the poets who settled in the Dymock–Ledbury area, his biased viewpoint shares common traits with the critics from the national press.

Here is part of an article from the *Gloucester Journal*, 12 January 1935:

> I cannot describe the splendour of his poems ... the more I read the book [*The Poems of Lascelles Abercrombie*] the more I am impressed by its colour, its imagination, its sense of character, its feeling for humanity, its visualisation of scenery, its humour, and above all, by its bigness and by its dignity, a bigness and dignity like that of Marlowe or Chapman or Marston ...

Abercrombie wrote large. He had access to 'otherness', and it was his otherness which gave the aura of greatness, if not its actuality in the end. For this reason, he is a useful case study in how a poet is perceived, and a good example of how an ambitious poet, confirmed in his vocation by influential reviews and a coterie ethos, can overreach his gift and negate those aspects of his art most likely to result in later success. A similar fate befell Wilfrid Gibson, as will be seen in chapter 2.

In order to understand Abercrombie's appeal to critics at the start of the twentieth century, we have to understand what the literary reader was used to seeing in the years around 1910, after Abercrombie's first collection (*Interludes and Poems*) was published, and before he joined forces with Marsh, Gibson and Brooke to forward the cause of new poetry. The fin de siècle was only ten years earlier, with arch-sensualist Swinburne still alive at the time of Abercrombie's breaking into print. People were used to the long poem in the late Romantic-Victorian manner, with Robert Bridges as the most famous poet of the new century, and narrative poets such as Alfred Noyes, Kipling and John Masefield providing a union between the 'thumping good read' and literary camps. Ezra Pound, despite being ubiquitous on the critical scene, was not widely read; and neither was Joyce, Lawrence, nor Eliot. Many of the difficulties associated with 'modernist' techniques did not yet exist in the minds of the critics, particularly for those born in the mid-Victorian period.

Literary education was still based upon the classics, with English only beginning to make its presence felt as a university subject – so the aspiring poet in 1905 was more likely to know about Greek metre and the epic vein rather than contemporary writing in modern Edwardian and Georgian English. This was something he had to discover for himself. Even Rupert Brooke, possibly the most forward of the poets examined here, felt compelled to experiment in choriambics rather than Imagism and vers-libre. In short, the turn of the century did not coincide with a rejection of what the previous century held dear, as though culture had turned a corner along with the millennium.

Abercrombie was therefore writing in an atmosphere still laden with trappings from the previous century, a background his academic frame of mind could hardly ignore. Ornateness, lengthy descriptions, subjects taken from the Bible and earlier legends, metaphysics: this is what Literature was made of, while the example of the rediscovered Elizabethans was there for all to see. Critics, even when they were of the calibre of Edward Thomas and Walter de la Mare, shared this classical–Romantic–Aesthetic background as a foundation for their own imaginative worlds, meaning that something impressive by Abercrombie was both recognizably poetic *and* new. He confronted intellectual issues and took inspiration from traditional sources, yet he was also capable of racy dialogue and humour; he was therefore a force to be reckoned with, a potential competitor for better-known narrative poets like John Masefield. When Abercrombie is viewed with historical hindsight, we know that his particular brand of vatic, dramatic poetry is 'oldfashioned' in comparison with the modernists and the pared-down, careful Georgianism of Thomas. But nobody knew this in 1908.

Moreover, nobody knew in 1908 that poetic drama – occasionally subjected to revivals – would never catch on with the theatregoing public in a sufficiently commercial way. This problem has particular relevance to Drinkwater's career, but it was Abercrombie whose discussions and polemic helped to push the art forward. He fervently believed in the future of poetic drama, and did not envisage its failure as a literary cul-de-sac. The following extract, taken from a lecture given at the Malvern Festival in 1934, indicates how he used to see poetic drama as part of a wider European movement, but is sadly speaking from the standpoint of an older, wiser man who has outgrown his earlier follies:

> When I was a young man, I had a great belief in the future of the poetic drama...I do not quite know why I believed the time had come...for poetic drama to blaze once more, Phoenix-like, into glorious theatrical life. But there were many who thought the same,

not only in England, but throughout Europe. And it seemed that our belief was not merely encouraged, but justified, by what was actually happening. There was Yeats in Ireland, D'Annunzio in Italy, Vertaeren in Belgium, Hauptmann in Germany, Rostand in France: a little later Gordon Bottomley in England. And there was also John Drinkwater.

In this atmosphere of pan-Europeanism, anything seemed possible. Georgian writing, whether through the medium of verse, drama, or a combination of the two, was shortly to be in the ascendant, with a supportive company at Birmingham Repertory Theatre willing to take the risk. Abercrombie's attachment to poetic drama was shared by several of his Georgian colleagues, and it is only our sceptical distance, seeing the resulting dramas in the context of Shaw and Ibsen, which places the Georgian experiment at a disadvantage.

Interludes and Poems (1908) sets out Abercrombie's position as a poet. Titles like 'The New God: A Miracle', and 'Indignation: An Ode' indicate how he is concerned with grand themes and stateliness. The opening of 'Ceremonial Ode' (subtitled 'Intended for a University') sounds as though it comes from Milton out of Wordsworth:

> When from Eternity were separate
> The curdled element
> And gathered forces, and the world began, –
> The Spirit that was shut and darkly blent
> Within this being, did the whole distress
> With blind desire after spaciousness.

Fortunately, this early tendency towards archaism, with poems liberally peppered with inversions and '-eth' forms, is only part of the picture. When writing in the guise of other characters, Abercrombie is interested in portraying how that character reacts and feels – he is not only concerned with poetic narrative. In 'Blind' (*IP* 39–78), a blind boy who is also a simpleton describes a recent event:

> Today, now,
> We met a little girl. My straying hands
> Found out her head; – there went a thrill in me,
> I'd found a new way of being pleased,
> Her hair. How I delighted all my feeling
> With touch of that strange fineness on my skin!

10

> But after, memory of that delight
> Wanted to put on words. And I had none
> For it to live in, and it ached in me.

Here, the poet has chosen to *inhabit* what it feels like to have unfamiliar experiences and unawakened emotion. The speaker does not know what is happening to him, and does not possess enough ability to describe what he is feeling. Abercrombie is writing as a character unlike himself, an intellectual destined for professordom with more than enough words at his disposal.

This ability to act and project in verse is what saves his dramatic poems from turgidity, and it was a talent soon recognized by the critics, as demonstrated in the quotation from the *Nation*. But the extract from 'Blind' points towards another strength, one not particularly highlighted at the time: Abercrombie's concern for intimate moments realized in precise language. This quieter, more lyrical mode is found elsewhere, as in the second stanza of the love poem 'All Last Night', also from his first collection:

> I knew the warmth in my dreaming;
> The fragrance, I suppose,
> Was her hair about me,
> Or else she wore a rose.

See also 'Roses Can Wound' (*PLA* 9).

Abercrombie's overall commitment to involving women in his poetry is another saving grace which prevents long works from containing predictable characters and stereotyped exchanges. Although his most widely publicized drama, *The End of the World*, takes place in a patriarchal rural society, his collected works show women envisaged as real people. They are not passive idols or femmes fatales, as in the Pre-Raphaelite/ Aesthetic traditions. Abercrombie's female characters include farm women, tramps and wanderers as well as princesses and saints; they have illegitimate children, are vociferous, witty and angry. Tennyson's Princess may have cried 'Sweet my child, I live for thee', but Abercrombie's females want to live for themselves – they have a robust attitude and an ability to voice their own needs. Even Mrs Huff, the one female character in *The End of the World*, is equal to the job when faced with two rival husbands:

11

> They thinking I'd be near one or the other
> After this night! Will I be made no more
> Than clay that children puddle to their minds,
> Moulding it what they fancy?

Unlike the male characters in this play, Mrs Huff relies on her own opinions and is not fooled by the behaviour of others.

When writing in his ornamental manner in 'The New God: A Miracle' (*IP* 3–35), Abercrombie provides us with another female capable of initiating action in a seemingly impossible situation. A Christian princess, trapped by the desire of a heathen prince and her father's intentions for the royal marriage market, evades them both as a result of her prayers. The poem ends without a statement of death or sacrifice, implying that she is spirited away temporarily rather than extinguished. Abercrombie derived his idea for this poem from a woodcut by Martin Schongauer (1453–91), showing his eclectic range of interests and background material.

His female characters may show vigorousness from the outset, but there is one problem area with 'The New God' which we find elsewhere, in *Mary and the Bramble* (1910). It involves conflict between what we perceive to be the environment of the people in the poems, and the actual environment which Abercrombie writes for them. In 'The New God', a situation of heathens versus Christians might suggest a remote past and a different country; Abercrombie sets the scene in 'Paynim, on the extreme coasts of the world'. Yet the landscape evoked in the poem is one of tarns, bogs, ploughland, apple orchards and 'upland hills', exactly the sort of landscape known to the Northerner poet who would soon relocate to the orchard district of north Gloucestershire. In *Mary and the Bramble*, published when Abercrombie had moved to Much Marcle, the Virgin Mary of the poem is not the one associated with hot, dry countries in the Middle East, but a woman who can walk in a 'meadow' and become entangled in a bramble thicket.

This discrepancy between the poet's intentions as an epic universalist poet and his particularized English landscape points out an underlying tension in his work, one which is not wholly explained by a comparison with the early visual arts technique of placing religious iconography in a contemporary setting. He is forcing himself to write in a certain way, and compromising on details which his artistic intelligence should have noticed. The effect is like that of seeing a period film where a leading character is wearing a wristwatch – we are left to gather from the overall context of the film whether the gesture was intentional. Abercrombie aspires towards Great Poetry, and falls short because he is composing too often with a pile of history books in the face of a genuine gift for relishing the countryside and its people. Few critics seem to have suspected him of artificiality and misdirection at the time, but Edward Thomas was conscious of his 'applying the lash', spurring on his poetic Pegasus to an artificial height.[5]

Mary and the Bramble, however, illustrates another noticeable feature. The Mary of the title becomes entangled in a bramble which is unusually menacing. It does not prick her and leave her to ponder on the nature of mortality, in the tradition of medieval verse. It accosts her, 'With eager thorns, tearing her dress to seize/ And harm her hidden white virginities'. The bramble is jealous of her future fame and immortality, something we can gather within a few lines. But Abercrombie lingers on the description, making us realize that the thorns cut deep:

> 'Ah, thy wicked daggers now
> Into my nipple cling:
> It is like guilt, so to be held
> In thy harsh fingering.'

The poem is as much about cruelty and jealousy as it is about religious fervour – and the feminist reader may wonder why the poet has chosen to describe religious/sexual harm at lurid length.

The character of Mary may seem unnecessarily suffering, yet Abercrombie visits an unnatural amount of suffering on his male character in 'Witchcraft – New Style' (*PLA* 296–300), proving that he does not envisage women as the sole gender to be acted upon. In this poem, a seemingly downtrodden woman, poor and old, has the power to control psychologically the man in her life, bringing him eternally running to her commands. The final section demonstrates Abercrombie's extravagance and Elizabethan panache:

> And there a man came running, a tall man
> Running desperately and slowly, pounding

> Like a machine, so evenly, so blindly;
> And regularly his trotting body wagg'd.
> Only one foot clattered upon the stones;
> The other padded in his dogged stride:
> The boot was gone, the sock hung frayed in shreds
> About his ankle, the foot was blood and earth;
> And never a limp, not the least flinch, to tell
> The wounded pulp hit stone at every step.
> His clothes were tatter'd and his rent skin showed,
> Harrowed with thorns. His face was pale as putty,
> Thrown far back; clots of drooping spittle foamed
> On his moustache, and his hair hung in tails,
> Mired with sweat; and sightless in their sockets
> His eyeballs turned up white, as dull as pebbles.
> Evenly and doggedly he trotted,
> And as he went he moaned. Then out of sight
> Round a corner he swerved, and out of hearing.

The poet has described an appearance of what is physically repellent, yet he has gone beyond the depiction of surfaces. The man apparently cannot feel his injured foot on the stones, and is incapable of stopping; he is in a kind of trance, showing the intensity of the old woman's grip over his mind, and Abercrombie's corresponding interest in fear, psychosis and punishment. J. W. Haines's rather gushing review in the *Gloucester Journal*, quoted at the beginning of this chapter, had enough prescience to recognize that his friend was capable of writing poetry that was 'weird and of the night'. The poet later regarded this poem as 'crude and dull' when it was published in *Georgian 4*, but, in its wild spinning into macabre territory, it is truly Abercrombiesque.

A set-piece of bloodiness and horror occurs also in *The Sale of St Thomas* (1911), a poem partially reproduced in Linda Hart's anthology (see bibliography), where Abercrombie describes the torture meted out to an early Christian missionary who cannot speak Indian languages. It is written with the same relish for detail as the extract provided above; a facility lacking in poems where Abercrombie is playing the role of philosopher-meta-physician. The poet was interested in ghost stories and the unseen, but this desire to capitalize on the pain of his characters may provide scope for investigation by a literary psychologist.

'Witchcraft – New Style' derives its strength from the gradual build-up towards the appearance of the bewitched man, placed as the climax at the end of the work. It is an effective use of a suspense mechanism, for the audience/reader wishes to know what kind of witchcraft is taking place, and how it is manifested in the man she controls; a power only suggested by her teasing comments to the rest of the cast. But this poem, set in a village pub and with characters drawn from the rural poor, derives its strength from its dialogue too:

> ...But he stood up to her awkwardly bold,
> One elbow on the counter, gripping his mug
> Like a man holding on to a post for safety.
> THE MAN   You can't do what's not nature: nobody can.
> THE WOMAN   And louts like you have nature in your pocket?
> THE MAN   I don't say that –
> THE WOMAN   If you kept saying naught,
> No one would guess the fool you are.

Here, they sound like 'real people' – particularly with the ungrammatical triple negative spoken by the man, a speech fitting his function in the poem as a loud uneducated bully. He seems uneasy too, an effect assisted by his awkward pose at the bar. His reaction is therefore what one would expect of a blustering man at the disadvantage of a sharper opponent.

The End of the World (1914) unites most of Abercrombie's positive aspects as a dramatic poet. It is published in its entirety in *Georgian Poetry 1913–15*, and it has potential in performance when approached by an inventive director. According to the *Birmingham Post* of 14 September 1914, the audience was disconcerted and unable to spot the humour in the play:

> the earnest-minded audience cheated itself out of considerable enjoyment by sitting with the gravity of mutes at a funeral. Much of the grim humour...went by unheeded in a wind of words.

The perceptive reviewer outlines and nails down the essential difficulty in Abercrombie's works:

> [his] men are alive, but they talk overmuch and labour at their thoughts like blacksmiths at a watchmaker's bench. A writer of discernment, of feeling, of power, many of his lines are clarions of revelation, but there were many tedious repetitions and variations on the same theme.

It invites the obvious conclusion that such an assemblage of obscure detail, 'wind', and repetition, would not result in many subsequent performances. Yet the play also contains rich colloquial language, with one person described as 'a grutchy mumchance fellow in the dismals' and another comparing the transience of life to 'a rotten toadstool kickt to flying bits'. *The End of the World* includes rustic speech worthy of Hardy, and does not proceed purely from an ability to write 'a wind of words'.

It was not the first Abercrombie drama to reach the stage, since *The Adder* was performed in Birmingham in 1912, provoking the review 'A morbid study of the aftermath of a life of sin which can produce nothing but a depressing effect' (*Post*, 19 May 1912). *The End of the World* tells the story of an itinerant dowser who alarms a village population by claiming that a visible comet is about to plummet to earth and destroy them all. The resulting uproar, involving drunkenness, wifeswapping and angry debate, is only resolved when the sign of a burning world is revealed to be a hayrick on fire in the distance; a discovery made by a passing molecatcher who enters the pub where the play is set. Order is restored, and two previously feuding villagers set out to find the dowser who has temporarily ruined their evening.

The atmosphere of the play is ostensibly one of bucolic comedy, but once again we can detect the Abercrombie concern for 'humour and horror tread[ing] a sinister saraband', as noticed by a *TLS* reviewer of *New Numbers* early in 1914. Abercrombie cranks up the language whenever an opportunity arises, and we are given the obligatory grisly set-piece where the dowser explains his compulsion to foretell doom, and the villagers' reply in kind:

STRANGER I have a sort of lust in me, pushing me still
Into that terrible way of thinking, like
Black men in India lie them down and long
To feel the holy wagon crack their spines.

MERRICK Do you mean beetles? I've driven over scores,
They sprawling on their backs, or standing mazed.
I never knew they liked it.

SOLLERS He means frogs.
I know what's in his mind. When I was young

> My mother would catch us frogs and set them down,
> Lapt in a screw of paper, in the ruts,
> And carts going by would squash 'em; and I'ld
>   laugh,
> And yet be thinking, 'Suppose it was myself
> Twisted stiff in huge paper, and wheels
> Big as the walls of a barn treading me flat!'

This frog-squashing incident angered critics in 1914 (see *GR* 149–51) and contributed more fuel to the debate of 'realism' in poetry, an issue central to Georgianism as originally conceived. Abercrombie was accused of deliberate nastiness, but nobody seems to have wondered why the incident was written. The villagers, unfamiliar with the Hindu 'juggernaut' driving over its extremist devotees, have to find the nearest equivalent from their own experience, which they translate as cruel boyhood games and the everyday spectacle of carts running over beetles in the road. There is a *reason* for the nastiness, and it is easier to justify in critical terms. *The End of the World* is a rare example of Abercrombie writing with consistency and care when approaching strangeness and nastiness, so that the poetic play works as a whole. In *The Sale of St Thomas* and 'Witchcraft – New Style', for example, the episodes of cruelty stand out like colour photographs inserted into a black and white album. They are foregrounded as a result of the poet exercising his talent, rather than being expressive of the theory and the circumstances of the entire drama.

In Abercrombie's output, it seems that 'realism' is confused with 'brutalism', an important distinction which paradoxically makes him appear more modern as a writer at the end of the century than he was at the start. Anyone who has seen a violent film or an experimental play will have no trouble accepting Abercrombie's 'nastiness' as literature. The problem with Abercrombie's poems is not that cruelty is described there, but that his neurotic form of realism creates conflicting registers of language within the same poem. At the end of the twentieth century, his is revealed as a structural problem rather than one of literary taste.

The End of the World can be read alongside Gordon Bottomley's *King Lear's Wife* in *Georgian Poetry 1913–15*, where we can see Edward Marsh's attempt to regenerate poetic drama along the lines of forcefulness and 'realism'. Bottomley outclasses Abercrombie in sustaining a dour, brutal atmosphere, a feature he extends to the invented names like Hygd (the Queen) and Gormflaith (a scheming maid). Due to a weak cast on the opening night at Birmingham Repertory Theatre, this play was doomed from the outset. But a large factor in the ultimate failure of both plays was the intervention of World War I, which changed the temper of the critics and the theatregoing public. They had no particular enthusiasm for plays foretelling the end of the world and the death of the old order.

Abercrombie became a successful academic after 1919, with several honours bestowed on him, a list of critical books in print, and lecture engagements overseas. But it would be wrong to regard him as a 'failed' poet, for, according to his contemporaries, he was nothing of the kind. When he returned to poetry after 1918, he possessed exactly the same facility and invention as before, as reported by Wilfrid Gibson in a letter to Walter de la Mare of 1 May 1919. His burst of activity in early 1919 resulted in such typically generous offerings as 'Ryton Firs' (*Georgian Poetry 1920–22*) a rhapsodic work based on the landmark firs around his old home near Dymock, felled for use as Welsh pit props during the First World War. Sections one and two of this discursive poem were written between 27 April and 3 May 1919, with section three ('The Dance') being a re-used text, written *c*.1913. The version published in *Georgian Poetry 1920–22* differs from the complete work published in the 1930 *Poems*, being only section two of a much longer piece. Abercrombie had wisely preceded this expansive section two, beginning 'Ryton Firs are alive again...' with the impact of quatrains, giving the modern, uncompromising appearance of a spoiled landscape:

> Dear boys, they've killed our woods: the ground
> Now looks ashamed, to be shorn so bare;
> Naked lank ridge and brooding mound
> Seem shivering cowed in April air.

This poem is worthwhile reading for those who are interested in the rural environment of the Dymock poets and what the landscape symbolized for them.

When assessing Abercrombie's contribution to Georgian poetry, it is helpful to look at his shorter poems for their lack

18

of artificial 'realism' and conscious literariness. The poet may have spent his energies on lengthy drama-poems, yet the engaging side of his art, more often found in archive letters than in the published drama, appears in poems such as 'The Stream's Song' (*PLA* 16–17), where a personified stream talks to the boulders it wears away:

> Crumble, crumble,
> Voiceless things;
> No faith can last
> That never sings.
>
> For the last hour
> To joy belongs;
> The steadfast perish,
> But not the songs.
>
> Yet for a while
> Thwart me, O boulders;
> I need for laughter
> Your serious shoulders.
>
> And when my singing
> Has razed you quite,
> I shall have lost
> Half my delight.

Like the stream, Abercrombie has set aside the cumbersome, archaic trappings holding him back. This poem was first published in 1911, with subsequent publication in *Twelve Idyls*, 1928. Despite the attractiveness of such lyrical, small-scale work, Abercrombie himself felt that long poetry was the only way to express his thoughts. This was not a result of egoism, but of his genuine love of the long poem, and his admiration for Hardy's *The Dynasts*, among others.

One more poem illustrates what might have been if Abercrombie had continued as a publishing poet instead of diverting his attention towards criticism during the 1920s. 'Epitaph', written when the poet was expecting to die as a result of complications brought on by diabetes, speaks to the reader out of cynicism and disillusion; traits associated with later poets rather than the Georgian alternative as it stood in 1914.

EPITAPH

Sir, you should notice me: I am the Man;
I am Good Fortune: I am satisfied.
All I desired, more than I could desire,
I have: everything has gone right with me.
Life was a hiding-place that played me false;
I croucht ashamed, and still was seen and scorned:
But now I am not seen. I was a fool,
And now I know what wisdom dare not know:
For I know Nothing. I was a slave, and now
I have ungoverned freedom and the wealth
That cannot be conceived: for I have Nothing.
I lookt for beauty and I longed for rest,
And now I have perfection: nay, I am
Perfection: I am Nothing, I am dead.

Keith Douglas (1920–44) and Sylvia Plath (1932–63) are recognized for writing about the simplification and perfection inherent in death – see, for instance, the lines 'Remember me when I am dead' by Douglas, written in 1941. Lascelles Abercrombie had covered much the same ground as Douglas, many years before.

It is easy to criticize Abercrombie for his failings as a pomp and circumstance writer, with his odes and idyls and three-act dramas. All of these are hard to categorize as modern, and today's reader must look carefully at his output for those signs of Georgianism and modernity which stand out so easily in other poets of the same period. Wilfrid Gibson, less intellectual than Abercrombie, was quicker at discovering his strong points as a poet and in exploiting them for a successful career. Abercrombie is an uneasy Georgian, despite his role as an insider with the Marsh circle and his eagerness as an initiator with *New Numbers*. Hampered by his academic love of old forms as well as his erratic control of realism, he is like the character in Matthew Arnold's 'Stanzas from the Grand Chartreuse', trapped as a poet 'between two worlds, one dead/ The other powerless to be born'. And when the new world finally broke over his head in 1914, his idiosyncratic old-world poetry became temporarily impossible for him to write.

2

Wilfrid Gibson
'Golden hearted through oblivion'

Wilfrid Gibson (1878–1962) belongs to the number of Georgians whose works 'pre-deceased' them, a problem realized by the poet himself as early as 1940. Unlike Abercrombie and Drinkwater, he did not have a secondary career, and in times of hardship he was almost completely dependent on the income provided by the Brooke legacy granted to him in 1915. He was born in Hexham, the son of a town chemist, and little is known about his early life. However, his poor eyesight and delicate constitution suggest a childhood susceptible to illness, and his education at the hands of his half-sister Elizabeth indicates a child who was considered unsuitable for the rough and tumble environment of the school playground. He was not intended for college, and he seems to have settled on his vocation as a poet early on, with short diversions as a social worker in Glasgow (1907) and London. It is likely that his literary ambitions were encouraged by Elizabeth, herself a poet with a modest amount of success. She was published by Elkin Mathews, who became Gibson's publisher in 1902. His background was secure enough and wealthy enough for him to avoid all serious forms of professional training, and it is easy to imagine a bookish, over-protected young man growing up in a provincial middle-class environment with few of the early pressures that hounded Edward Thomas and John Drinkwater.

Gibson was, however, a sociable character; and his mild, clerkly demeanour went hand in hand with a genius for friendship and an open, good-humoured manner. People were drawn to him, and he was a generous and often hilarious correspondent. Hundreds of extant letters show his clear, wrily amused attitude towards life; and while his poetry may have fallen out of favour, Gibson the personality remained popular. His relations with the other 'Dymock Poets' were not always straightforward, but it is possible to build up a more accurate picture of his subdued but likeable character from the numerous correspondences which survive outside the Dymock enclave.

His career as a poet was assisted greatly by the inspiration provided by his wife, Geraldine Audrey Townshend, whom he married in 1913. She was a prime homemaker as well as a lively personality, and Gibson was besotted – any poem with the dedication 'For G.' or 'To G.' invariably means Geraldine. His contented relationship is commemorated in several poems, including the very specific 'For G' (CP 344, sometimes known as 'All Night Under the Moon') where Gibson expresses his love both of Geraldine and the thatched cottage at Greenway, near Dymock, where they lived between 1913 and 1916:

> All night under the moon
> Love, though we're lying
> Quietly under the thatch in the silvery light
> Over the meadows of June
> Together we're flying
> Rapturous voices of love in the hush of the night.

Gibson wrote a variation of this poem in *Home* (CP 518–19), entitled 'The Empty Cottage'.

On the whole, Gibson led a suburban life after 1919, when he left Malvern for the Home Counties. He spent most of the next forty-two years around Hertfordshire and Surrey, with a brief sojourn in London between 1933 and 1939 in closer proximity to the literary opportunities offered by the capital. He died in a nursing home at Virginia Water in 1962, leaving a large body of poetic work and an artistic reputation which had levelled off and slowly turned downhill after his *Collected Poems* were published by Macmillan in 1925. Gibson's longevity and his tendency to repeat himself meant that in the light of subsequent poetic 'movements' he had apparently outlived his moment. Yet his artistic reputation had once been at the highest level possible for a poet, with an extended reading tour of the United States culminating in the American edition of his collected poetry being published in 1917 when the poet was barely halfway through his writing career. As late as 1933 he had a reading tour schedule which included Liverpool, Oxford, Manchester

Scotland, London and 'The North', causing him to remark, 'I'm through with public appearances for this year – thank goodness'.[1] Gibson was almost a casualty of his own success, with his early reputation as a 'people's poet' being one of the first to suffer, eclipsed by intellectual writers whose audience consisted of influential editors and other intellectuals rather than 'the people'.

The shifting ground of the early twentieth-century poetry market explains why Gibson does not feature in many literary histories other than those particularly Georgian. This means that his striking short poems are denied to the contemporary audiences who are more attuned to cross-cultural entertainment and a plurality of literary styles. Readers of performance poetry and romantic sagas may even find that *Krindlesyke* (1922) and *Kestrel Edge* (1924) are well worth reading for their entertainment value alone; the populist genre of Northern writing appropriated by Catherine Cookson was a genre first exploited by Wilfrid Gibson.

The last sentence may sound surprising, but it is noticeable that Gibson started from the position of a romancer in poetry, and that the idea of the saga and the nature of human relationships form two of the major themes in his later poetic and dramatic works. His earliest volumes, including *The Golden Helm* (1902), have been described as Tennysonian, but it would be more accurate to describe them as Rossetti–Morris in their idealized medievalism. The following example shows his typical subject matter, written before a growing commitment to social issues drove him to work in the slums of Glasgow in 1907. It is taken from 'The Vision', a romance about the conflict between the appeal of Arthurian legend and the reality as represented by Western Christianity:

> The white lily, Guenevere,
> Ruthless time has trodden down;
> Arthur is a tarnished crown,
> High Gawain a broken spear,
> Percival a riven shield;
> They, who taught the world to yield,
> Closed with death and lost the field,
> Stricken by the last despair:
> Launcelot is but a name

> Blown about the winds of shame;
> Surely God has quenched the flame
> That burned men's souls for Guenevere.

At 24, Gibson could write serviceable medievalist verse. He was originally a historicist poet, sharing the same archaic interests as his early Georgian colleagues, who found the past a difficult country to escape from. Gibson was later able to indulge his romance interests in torrid Northumbrian verse dramas, where his love of literary language could find expression in Northern colloquialisms instead of poetic stereotypes. The North is a constant presence in Gibson's work, and he claimed that the austerity of the high fell country with its expanses of heather and running stone walls meant more to him than any other landscape.

The precise reasons for Gibson's change of style c.1907 are unknown. The medieval-verse writer emerged from his chrysalis as a 'people's poet' in 1908, thereafter choosing folk anecdotes, real life and the labouring poor as his subject matter. Some of this *volte face* must have occurred through his work in Glasgow, which in turn was probably fired by an increasing desire to participate in society; Gibson's world prior to that date seems suspiciously home-bound and insular. Literary reasons may also have played a part in his decision to change styles – it is likely that King Arthur seemed no longer relevant to the adult man in 1906, one determined to make his career as a writer, but with few income-gaining strategies. Writing about 'real life' at least guaranteed a wider audience, as John Masefield would discover in 1911 after the publication of *The Everlasting Mercy*. Whatever his real reasons were, Gibson's change in style catapulted him from being a Northern chemist's son with a few oldfashioned verses in print to being a challenging new British writer. Reviews, often the best promotion a poet could have in the days before the mass media, show the emotional impact Gibson could have, and the appeal of his narrative verse to the general public. In the following extracts, Gibson is perceived as a naturalistic writer, a democrat with insight and a social conscience:

> the purified simplicity of common speech which Mr. Gibson uses avoids anything like the effect of a style imposed, and very strongly gives the effect of substance naturally manifesting itself in style. We may as well admit here which side we are on; these narratives and

dramas seem to us unquestionably poetry of a very moving and impressive kind. (*TLS*, 8 May 1913)

Since *Daily Bread* other books have appeared – *Fires*, in 1912, *Womenkind* in 1913, and *Borderlands* and *Thoroughfares* in 1914. In each there has been the same penetrating insight into the psychology of social misery, the same prophetic understanding of the wants and woes of submerged men, the same august revelation of the secrets of the heart that is robbed of its heritage of love. (*The Survey*, 6 January 1917)[2]

Unlike Abercrombie, he was not an intellectual in verse, and he was less uneven as a narrative writer; unlike much of Thomas's poetry, his work was concerned with the problems of other people rather than his own temperament – and unlike Brooke, he was not interested in cruelly satirizing his subjects. He therefore reads as a compassionate and humane writer, a condition of his art which acted to his advantage as a writer of war verse who did not serve in France. He achieved his grasp of other characters by a Keatsian 'negative capability', identifying with what he heard and saw outside himself, but without participating directly in the events he describes. This led him to rely overmuch on reminiscence and anecdote in his total output, but at his best Gibson is a sensual writer, alive to the sounds and textures of the environments he is creating. His sensuousness in verse is demonstrated by his often anthologized 'The Ice Cart' (*CP* 342), where a bored office worker imagines himself in an arctic landscape:

> Until I stumbled unawares
> Upon a creek where big white bears
> Plunged headlong down with flourished heels
> And floundered after shining seals
> Through shivering seas of blinding blue.
> And, as I watched them, ere I knew
> I'd stripped and I was swimming too
> Among the seal-pack, young and hale,
> And thrusting on with threshing tail,
> With twist and twirl and sudden leap
> Through crackling ice and salty deep,
> Diving and doubling with my kind...

Gibson was realistic and often self-deprecating about his literary talent, and he left no indications that he was a tortured artist. He was as much of a 'writing animal' as Edward Thomas, dependent on an income from literary work, but his character seems to have been naturally sunny and optimistic beneath the domesticated exterior. His letters[3] state that he was a boom and bust writer, often going for months without creating any poetry, then suddenly being pitched into a ferment of writing. Writing did not come easily to him, even though his boom periods resulted in fluent work – he found it hard to distinguish between good and bad poetry, mistrusted his inspiration, and was less than satisfied with his lines. He was a hard worker too; 'Makeshifts' (*Livelihood*, 1916) has survived in seven drafts, beginning with a three-page fragment entitled 'Hugh'. The resulting length of the retitled poem averages at sixteen pages. His writing was derived from the typical creative struggle endured by many artists, although Gibson himself appears to have been floating serenely on the surface in his everyday life.

His modesty regarding his own talent is expressed in a comment he made while touring the USA in 1917, where he told the assembled professors of the University of Chicago that he was not very familiar with metre and versification. This is patently untrue, judging by Gibson's writings from his earliest period; in the university context, he must have meant that he was unfamiliar with the academic reasoning processes and classical terminology employed by his hosts. In short, his unpretentious lyrics and narratives stemmed from a personality which did not affect artistic superiority or special knowledge. This is one reason why writers and critics of all types found him an endearing man. Poets as diverse as Brooke and Frost regarded him as a great friend (although the latter changed his opinion in 1914, and in later life, he struck up a friendship with W. H. Auden, who gave him invaluable advice on attracting large fees.[4] The Georgian who was out of sympathy with later twentieth-century styles had little difficulty in communicating with one of the most strident heralds of modernism.

In 1912, Gibson left Hexham for London, seeking fame as a writer. He already had ten short volumes in print, and good literary contacts in the metropolis. For part of 1912–13 he found employment as the assistant editor of *Rhythm* (later *The Blue Review*), run by John Middleton Murry and Katherine Mansfield. He did not know that his wages were paid in a circuitous way by Edward Marsh, who contributed financially to the enterprise when times were hard. In 1913, Gibson lodged in the rooms provided by Harold Monro above the Poetry Bookshop, where he was in the best position to meet the London writers who attended the weekly Thursday evening readings. Gibson first met Geraldine on the staircase at Monro's establishment, an incident recalled in 'The Stair' (*CP* 518) – it must be the only example of a poet being provided with a publisher, a room, and a wife, on the same premises in that order. However, Gibson's relationship with Monro soon suffered a setback, when the plans for *New Numbers* went ahead as Gibson intended. Incredibly, Monro took offence, accusing him of stealing Geraldine so that Monro's own Georgian anthologies would be worse off without her useful assistance. This point illustrates how claustrophobic the Georgian publishing world could be; *New Numbers* was only one of several anthologies, following in the wake of *Georgian Poetry 1911–12*, which saturated the available market and contributed to the demise of Marsh's literary empire.

Gibson's poetic output can be divided into three types: books of short lyrics (*Whin, Battle*) narrative verse (*Stonefolds, Fires*) and poetic drama (*Krindlesyke*). Of the latter, Gibson did not envisage stage production, and he did not think of himself as a playwright, despite his ability to portray characters equipped with motivation and distinguishing speech patterns. Drinkwater, who made his acquaintance before 1911, tried to persuade him to write for the stage, but Gibson regarded it as a wrong direction despite seeing his works presented by actors more than once. 'Hoops' (1914) was performed as part of a triple bill with Brooke's *Lithuania* and Bottomley's *King Lear's Wife*, at a Georgian matinée directed by Drinkwater at His Majesty's Theatre, London, in May 1916.

Gibson's ambitions were confined to the written page, and he did not share the same love of the stage as his Georgian friends. Nevertheless, a work such as 'Bloody Bush Edge' (1914) could make effective radio material, with its ability to convey character through dialogue. This was a particular talent of Gibson's; compare the clownish, camp traveller Albert Edward Higgs, depicted in 'Red Rowan' (*Gangrels*, 1924). 'Bloody Bush Edge' is set in a real location close to the Scottish borders, and it is a dialogue between a vagrant ('Daft Dick') and an unnamed traveller from London. We work out gradually that the latter is a criminal on the run, but Daft Dick is not so daft, telling ghost stories about the district in a deliberate attempt to get rid of his unwelcome visitor. He succeeds, and is able to continue his solitary life without further interference. Part of his success is due to the guilt complex exhibited by the London visitor, who is in such a state of nervous tension that he is ready to believe the horror stories told to him. 'Bloody Bush Edge' was first published in *New Numbers*, issue number 1, contributing greatly to the racy new style envisaged by the first Georgians. A comparison of Gibson material between 1908 and 1922 and some of the older Georgians promoted by Marsh and Monro shows that he was one of the closest adherents to the anti-Victorian style in poetry, anticipating Masefield in his desire to delve into the problems of the poor and dispossessed. Sometimes, as in 'Bloody Bush Edge', Gibson keeps his tragic note in check; but it is true to describe him as a tragedian, one who is able to catch the reader out with unexpected shafts of comedy.

'The Stone' (*Fires*, 1912) is typical of Gibson's narrative verse. It uses plain language, a strong emotional appeal, and tragic subject matter based on the lot of the labouring poor. In this poem, a stonemason is given an assignment for a headstone, only to find himself adding a second name at the end of the work. The unnamed girl who gave the commission has died of a broken heart. Gibson's closeness to folk literature is illustrated by the quatrain at the start of the poem, which sounds like a folksong verse:

> *And will you cut a stone for him,*
> *To set above his head?*
> *And will you cut a stone for him –*
> *A stone for him?* she said.

He goes on to describe an accident in a quarry: 'Three days before a splintered rock/ Had struck her lover dead', before relating what happened next, in true storyteller's fashion:

> I went to break the news to her,
> With dread of what my lips might say;

28

But some poor fool had sped before
And, flinging wide her father's door,
Had blurted out the news to her,
Had struck her lover dead for her,
Had struck the girl's heart dead in her,
Had struck life lifeless at a word
And dropped it at her feet,
Then hurried on his witless way
Scarce knowing she had heard.
And when I came she stood alone –
A woman turned to stone,
And though no word at all she said,
I knew that all was known.

(CP 154–5)

Gibson is more artful than his poems often suggest. In the extract above, the girl becomes like a stone in a typical artistic conceit. Later, in another metaphorical conceit, the stonemason is an agent of death, conspiring to kill the girl: 'The two of us were chiselling/ Together, I and death'. But the stonemason is a vehicle for empathy too – he regrets the clumsy way in which the girl was informed of the tragedy. He is a participant in a community, not merely an unnamed workman with a job to do. We can also see some justification in the promotional statement made by the publisher of *Fires* in 1912: 'He is a master in terse, vivid phrases and in the harmony of discords'.

Other works are not so lucky in their ability to survive the test of time. Gibson can appeal to popular sentiment with a too heavy hand, resulting in maudlin, pot-boiler material. 'The Blind Rower', also from *Fires*, is a doleful Northern tale involving a man who has died in a rowing boat while his blind son is rowing him home. The reader's common sense soon asks why the blind son could not hear his father having a stroke in the close environment of a rowing boat; Gibson the seeker of pathos asks too much of the reader's willing suspension of disbelief.

Gibson's numerous short books of lyrical poetry quickly reveal him as a thematic writer – many poets build their books around one or two themes, but with Gibson the titles alone give the readers all they need to know about the likely contents: *Friends, Battle, Casualties, Neighbours*. On a less positive note, his ability to write a book around a theme, as if he had said to

29

himself 'I will set out to write a number of poems about my neighbours', can highlight his drawback in writing from the outside, as one who drives his subject matter rather than being driven by it. Both Frost and Thomas recognized this quality in Gibson at the time, and his journalistic view of the world as subject matter has contributed to some of the flatness and repetition found in his less successful work. Other critics, too, were not without reservations. They 'questioned whether his chief characteristics, colloquialism and symbolism, could go together' (Obituary, *The Times*, 28 May 1962). Elsewhere, Gibson's lyrical purity and closeness to the folksong tradition made his verses attractive to Georgian composers, in particular Herbert Howells (1892–1983), who set six poems from *Whin* during 1918 and 1919.

Battle (1915) demonstrates the concision and colloquialism which Gibson was famous for during his lifetime. Remarkably, *Battle* was written by a poet who never saw the trenches; Gibson's eyesight was too poor for active service overseas. He failed the necessary medical tests five times, although he was able to serve as a clerk in the Army Service Corps during 1918. Nevertheless, he was able to empathize with the conditions of those in the trenches, and he was able to express the shock of death, injury, and the psychological strain which resulted in mental breakdown for so many of the active participants. Gibson's poems are low-key, meaning that they do not have the political impact of those by Owen and Sassoon, but they should be read alongside those by the 'trench poets' for their contribution to be fully recognized. Here is part of an extensive review published by the *TLS* in 1916, under the title 'An Ironist of the Trenches':

> The little book is a monument to the wantonness of it all, to the cheapness of life in war, the carelessness as to the individual, the disregard alike of promise and performance, the elimination of personality...Mr. Gibson speaks for the perplexed soldier under orders, and in doing so, illustrates the other side of the medal. In war, he says, in effect, there are no longer men, there is no longer man, there are only sports of chance, pullers of triggers, bewildered fulfillers of instructions, cynical acceptors of destiny.

This anti-heroic attitude is closer in spirit to the post-1918 perception of war, bearing little resemblance to the heroic outrage of the public-school poet, Siegfried Sassoon. The following two complete poems show Gibson's achievements in *Battle*. In the first, we hear his ability to voice the worries of ordinary, unsophisticated soldiers, and his economy at suggesting the background of his speakers:

HIS FATHER

I quite forgot to put the spigot in:
It's just come over me...And it is queer
To think he'll not care if we lose or win,
And yet be jumping-mad about that beer.

I left it running full. He must have said
A thing or two. I'd give my stripes to hear
What he will say if I'm reported dead
Before he gets me told about that beer!

(CP 326)

Although this poem is brief, we learn something about the speaker and his father, with its indication of a tricky relationship. In the second poem, Gibson shows his concern for the lasting trauma of going to war with one's fellow man:

BACK

They ask me where I've been,
And what I've done and seen.
But what can I reply
Who know it wasn't I,
But someone just like me,
Who went across the sea
And with my head and hands
Killed men in foreign lands...
Though I must bear the blame,
Because he bore my name.

(CP 327)

Here, the dissociation of the man from his actions is true to the dilemma of the unwilling soldier, acting the role of a killing machine while suppressing his humanitarian feelings.

Gibson's psychological angle on poetry can help his output become 'modern' even though his work fell out of favour after 1925. 'In The Wood', from *Beauty for Ashes* (c.1923) is about a lack of communication between two people, with that 'something

31

else' recurring as a refrain, serving to worry the writer and the subsequent reader.

IN THE WOOD

The day you came upon us in the wood
You said no word but only glanced at me,
And then went on to talk of something else.

How could I tell you you'd misunderstood
When you – you said no word of it to me,
But talked so steadily of something else?

If you had only spoken out I could
Have told you all and you forgiven me,
But you thought best to talk of something else.

Because your heart was troubled you thought good
To say no word about it and spare me:
So we must always talk of something else.

(CP 781)

This is only one of the many intimate poems which Gibson could create with style and conviction. It is no more conventionally 'Georgian' than the poetry of Frost or Brooke, and it transcends its circumstances in postwar 1920s Britain.

Krindlesyke (1922) marked a high point in Gibson's career, according to critics at the time. It received impressive praise, including the following hyperbole by Abercrombie, later quoted in a small edition of selected poems issued in 1931 by Ernest Benn (see bibliography):

No poetry of our time appeals more surely to the infinite possibilities of human nature, no poetry exhibits more of the beauty human nature is capable of in its triumph over reality. This is the wealth Mr. Gibson finds everywhere; and his finding it can transfigure the drabbest event.

In a concise assessment of the same work, the *Southport Guardian* of 28 April 1923 describes it as having 'amazing vitality and amazing violence'. Abercrombie's excitement over *Krindlesyke* centres on Gibson's ability to make his characters survivors over circumstances. It is the drama of the spiritual struggle which impresses him, and for Abercrombie, poetry and beauty are synonymous with dramatic potential and metaphysical issues. Yet *Krindlesyke* is melodrama in a traditional sense, with its

32

rampant householders, wronged women, and gipsy interlopers. Readers of historical romance, particularly those works set in remote country districts like the novels of Mary Webb, will be familiar with most of the situations encountered in *Krindlesyke*, which began life as a music-hall play, *Womenkind*, in 1913.

The book is divided into three parts, 'Phoebe Barrasford', 'Krindlesyke', and 'Bell Haggard'. It is about several generations of life in a harsh Northumberland farmstead, whose name gives the book its title. In this saga, Gibson gives full rein to his interest in dialect and emotive language, with the character of Ezra in 'Phoebe Barrasford' showing how far he could go in terms of retaining minimal amounts of orthodox structure in order to make the speech intelligible. The sample speech given here comes after Jim (Ezra's son) has just received a shock in the form of his old girlfriend, Judith, who has arrived at Krindlesyke with his baby. Phoebe (newly married to Jim) decides to leave with Judith rather than remain with her husband.

> EZRA   I can't make head or tail of all the wrangling –
> Such a gillaber and gilravishing
> As I never heard in all my born days, never.
> Weddings were merrymakings in my time:
> The reckonings didn't come till the morrow's morn.
> But Jim, my boy, though you're a baa-waa body
> And gone about like a goose with a nicked head,
> You've aiblains found out now that petticoats
> Are kittle-cattle, the whole rabblement.
> The reesty nags will neither heck nor gee;
> And they're all cling-clang like the Yetholm tinkers.
> Ay, though you're just a splurging jackalally,
> You've spoken truth for once, Jim – women folk,
> Wenches and wives, are all just weathercocks.
> I've ever found them faithless, first and last.

(CP 551)

This speech is characteristic of Gibson in his Northern-Fantasy style; vivid, expressive, and more than a little comic. In 'Bell Haggard', Gibson piles on the grim Northern reality until we wonder whether he can possibly be serious. In the extract here, Bell is remembering the burial of an old miserly relative who died while counting fifty imaginary gold pieces; he died on the count of forty-nine.

JUDITH   Ay, but it's sad
            When the wits go first.

BELL   And he so wried and geyzened
            The undertakers couldn't strake him rightly.
            Even when they'd nailed him down, and we were watching
            By candle-light the night before the funeral
            Nid-nodding, Michael and I, just as the clock
            Struck twelve there was a crack that brought us to
            Bolt upright as the coffin-lid flew off
            And old granddaddy sat up in his shroud.

JUDITH   God save us, woman! Whatever did...

BELL   I fancied
            He'd popped up to say fifty; but he dropped back
            With knees to chin. They'd got to screw him down:
            And they'd sore work to get him underground –
            Snow overnight had reached the window sill;
            And when at length the cart got on the road
            The coffin was jolted twice into the drifts
            Before they'd travelled the twelve mile to the
                churchyard:
            And the hole they'd howked for him, chockful of slush;
            And the coffin slipped with a splash into the sluther.
            Ay, we see life at Krindlesyke, God help us!

                                            (CP 571)

Stella Gibbons's *Cold Comfort Farm* (1932) is a holiday resort compared to Krindlesyke and the equally undesirable residence, Windwhistle, from *Kestrel Edge* (1924). Gibson's dramas owe a great deal to folk traditions and proletarian literature, but this should not limit their appeal – their large-scale themes of love and death are those found universally, and in their potential for an immediate impact they are never dull. Ezra's speech (see page 33) points to a collective misogyny in some of the 'menfolk', but on the whole Gibson portrays survivor women with dignity and emotion – the active daughters and characterful elders who are noticeable in the Georgian dramas of Edward Marsh's associates.

Gibson's personal modesty and his tendency to live a suburban life after 1919 militates against his image as a poet. There is a tendency for readers and critics, accustomed to the cult of biography, to regard artists as people with extraordinary private lives or adventurous dispositions which somehow inform their creative works. At least two of the Georgians in this study belong to that category, but Gibson is resistant to all forms of image making and publicity, with his early high reputation based on the solid foundations of a great deal of work. By contrast, Brooke's reputation was founded on his icon value; his output of poetry was both small and slow during his lifetime. Gibson's status as a poet during the Georgian era was entirely due to his commitment to the desk and the paper tray, with several excellent poems such as 'The Ice Cart' making their way into the national consciousness as forcefully as Brooke's 'The Soldier'. Literary fashions may have moved on too quickly for that status to be retained, but with historical hindsight, Gibson can be reassessed as a necessary writer for his generation. The final word belongs to J. W. Haines, who had plenty of opportunities to observe Gibson the writer while associating with him in Gloucestershire:

> I have always found in reading poetry to public audiences that his poetry went down better than anyone's. He writes of character and circumstance, dramatic tales which all humanity can understand and enjoy, a class of poetry which has its glorious English origin in Chaucer.[5]

3

Edward Thomas
'Putting in the seed'

Edward Thomas (1878–1917) is now one of the best-loved twentieth-century poets, whose influence has spread ripples in the creative pond far greater than the small amount of poetry he wrote ever did during his lifetime. He was regarded as 'the father of us all' by Ted Hughes,[1] and, considered as a Georgian associate in his lifetime, he can be seen as responsible for rescuing the quiet, personal style from triviality and sterility. Thomas's countryside is one where the walker can feel lost and threatened, and there are ramifications beyond the words on the page. It is possible to read matters into his poetry in a way that one cannot do with Gibson and Drinkwater, making Thomas a culturally rich experience beyond his time, whereas Gibson and Drinkwater are irretrievably stuck in theirs. He is not obvious, no matter how plain his verse may seem; he is spiritual, but not in a religiose, churchy way; he is an observer, but his powers of observation put him closer to his subject matter than the poetry of those who work from an external stimulus. His posthumous reputation immediately begs the question of why he took so long to realize his poetic ambitions, when even a friend of relatively short acquaintance, like Robert Frost, could see that he was wasting his talents on the wrong kinds of literature.

Thomas's biography is well known compared to those of other Georgians, so there is less need to repeat facts which can easily be gained from literary histories and the prefaces to modern editions. But what is not generally known is the difficulty Thomas had in formulating his own character in the first place, meaning that his long evolving towards poetry is not only symptomatic of the man, but might have been a good deal shorter if he had followed his original instincts. A collection of letters to Harry Hooton in the Bodleian Library[2] gives details of Thomas the undergraduate as he was in 1897–9 and the picture as it stood before he embarked on married life and a full-time writing career. Thomas the young aesthete was quite different from the remote melancholic with the black moods and family tensions which became noticeable in his later life. In his letters to Hooton, he is a highly impressionable man, oversensitive and emotional to a surprising extent. He was drawn towards other people with a schoolboy's infatuation, while at the same time forming a deep relationship with Helen Noble, the daughter of his literary mentor James Ashcroft Noble. But while Helen turned out to be the ideal partner, his own personality was in such a state of flux that he felt compelled to remodel himself in an effort to combat his emotionalism and what he described as 'feminine' characteristics. And the model he chose was unfortunately that of a repressed Englishman, something he would ruefully acknowledge later in the lines 'I Built Myself A House of Glass' (1915):

> I built myself a house of glass:
> It took me years to make it:
> And I was proud. But now, alas,
> Would God someone would break it.

By forcing himself to live up to an English stereotype, instead of working through his prolonged 'aesthetic' adolescence like other young men, he cut off areas of his psyche as though he was a tree with unwanted branches, and possibly sowed the seeds of his later difficulties. His family and trusted friends would see the 'real' Thomas, capable of lightheartedness and openness, but the less fortunate might encounter the Marsh version as reported by Hassall in *Edward Marsh*:

> It must have been one of his less good days – he was unforthcoming and constricted, perhaps dyspeptic, and seemed to look down his nose at both of us as well as the food, so it led to nothing. I wish we could have met him in the country and known the man you describe. (*EM* 211)

The above quotation illustrates what we can gather about Thomas from other sources. He has a hatred of the smart London set and the necessity of cultivating their approval, and there is the suspicion that his character is highly variable despite the constriction. Worst of all, Thomas is aloof, yet without the means to meet his audience halfway, not even when encountering a dedicated, classless promoter of the arts like Edward Marsh. This, combined with his diffidence and a job which involved promoting himself to hard-nosed editors who already had other writers on their lists, made Thomas seem like a man frequently at odds with his environment. When the situation became intolerable at home, Thomas would erupt into a 'wild Shelleyan creature',[3] and terrify both Helen and little Merfyn.

Thomas had, of course, aggravated his situation in more ways than the psychological one. He had rejected his father's suggestion of a career in the Civil Service, seemingly unaware that he could have earned a few years' worth of income before cutting loose into the literary life. Ironically, he was forced to seek office employment in 1908, although his five month post with the Royal Commission for Welsh Monuments was unsuccessful. He had determined to earn his living by his pen before he had left Oxford, and unwittingly shackled himself to a constant treadmill of reviews, biographies, and topographical books. Some of these were dictated by personal interests, such as his biographies of Richard Jefferies (1909) and Walter Pater (1911), but most were regarded as hack work, written to deadlines and achieved within weeks rather than months or years. The disembodied hand crawling across the page in 'The Long Small Room' (1916, *CPET* 122) suggests the dispiriting, eternal grind which Thomas endured for most of his prose career.

By 1913 he was a sought-after reviewer for the *Daily Chronicle* and elsewhere, regarded as an essential critic for new poetry, with an ability to make or break reputations. He was well known in literary circles despite his reticence, and he was the author of British topographical works in an era when the industrial classes were discovering the great outdoors. His books did not receive universal praise or the benefit of huge sales, but the London slums where he first lived with Helen in 1900 were far behind him, and he was able to live in the countryside he loved. His opinions of other Georgians were favourable, and there are approving comments concerning Brooke, Abercrombie, W. H. Davies and de la Mare scattered through his correspondence. He was credited with 'discovering' Davies, who wrote *Autobiography of a Supertramp* (1908) at his suggestion. But he described Drinkwater as 'hopeless' and Gibson nearly as bad, in a letter to John Freeman (January 1915) when Thomas himself had begun to write poetry. His blind spot regarding Gibson – an opinion shared by Helen Thomas – remained, despite several meetings at Dymock during the summer of 1914. Both men must have been conscious of this failure in understanding, and Thomas had already made his opinions publicly known in 1912, when he reviewed *Fires* as prosaic and journalistic (*Daily Chronicle*, 9 March). Thomas the critic was impressed by quality and integrity rather than schools of thought and group machinations, and he astonished literary London by writing a positive review of Ezra Pound's *Personae* in the *English Review*, June 1909. The arch-enemy of little Englandism was placed on the British poetry scene by the foremost Georgian critic.

A combination of factors led Thomas towards poetry. Firstly, there was the enormous amount of contemporary verse which he read and reviewed for money; few poets could have started with such a natural advantage of background knowledge and critical insight. Secondly, he had several friends who tried to persuade him that his talents were being used wrongly, and that he ought to write poems. Robert Frost is acknowledged as the 'only begetter', but Gordon Bottomley, John Freeman, Walter de la Mare, and Eleanor Farjeon had already raised the matter with him. The problem seems to have been Thomas's acute lack of confidence, and an inability to act on his deepest desires and instincts. In effect, he had frozen out a literary talent which his friends could recognize as dispersed among his writings on countryside subjects. At the same time, some of his comments are like those of a man who *wants* to be told 'yes you can do it', in their desire for a direct response:

> I wonder whether you can imagine me taking to verse. If you can I imagine I might get over the feeling that it is impossible – which it once obliges your good nature to say 'I can'. In any case, I must have my 'writer's melancholy' though I quite agree with you that I might spare some of it to the deficient. . . . I go on writing something every day. Sometimes brief unstrained impressions of things lately seen . . . Is this North of Bostonism?

These extracts, written to Frost before Thomas's influential summer with Frost at Ledington and Oldfields in 1914, show that he was already on the way towards becoming a poet. He almost jokingly refers to his 'writer's melancholy' as though he knows the cause and relies on it for an excuse not to start. Above all, he *needs* Frost to say 'Yes' – this will give him the signal he requires to overcome the obstacle he has given himself. For Thomas had always wanted to be a poet; he wrote verses while at Oxford, but he regarded these attempts as laughable and the art too difficult for him to master. Significantly, he recognized early on that some of his prose writings should be in verse, as he outlined this to Harry Hooton in a letter dated 24 November 1897.

However, the obstacle was not only within Thomas. His need for a regular income meant that he was hard at work as a prose writer, and unlike those poets who could retire to the study after a day at the office, he was unable to release himself. He was on the go constantly, walking the landscape in search of material, and reviewing as many as twenty books in a week. Some poets, such as Robert Graves, could operate the prose/poetry switch without too much difficulty; but this was impossible for the overworked Thomas. Conducive social factors were necessary before Thomas could focus his attention on poetry, and these did not happen until late 1914 when the supply of reviewing work began to dry up and the nation turned to war. The same circumstances which drove Abercrombie into the munitions industry assisted Thomas with his important decision. Once he had enlisted in 1915, the regular pay and freedom from intellectual strain meant that he had the mental space for composition, as opposed to the physical space he had enjoyed in the country, which did not always go hand in hand with intellectual freedom.

After Thomas's favourable review of Frost's *A Boy's Will* in 1913, the two corresponded and became friends. Frost (1874–1963) had been a temporary resident in England since 1912, after deciding to kick-start his career as a poet in the UK rather than wait any longer in America. He was 39, five years older than Thomas, with a body of unpublished work behind him, and only a few poems in print. *A Boy's Will* was published in London by the respectable firm of David Nutt, most probably at the suggestion of John Drinkwater, who acted as a reader for the company. In 1914 this was followed by *North of Boston*, and Frost's reputation was established. He returned to America as a poet in 1915, but not before he had persuaded Thomas to follow his example.

Much of this persuasion would have taken place in the countryside around Dymock and Ledington, where the poets were staying in August 1914. Frost was at Little Iddens, three fields away from the Thomases at Oldfields, with the houses connected by a public footpath. Over a period of four weeks, the two men roamed the countryside and outlined their theories of contemporary poetry. Thomas was impressed above all by Frost's revolutionary refusal to use overtly poetical constructions. In *North of Boston* he found his 'language not to be betrayed': it was 'free from the poetical words and forms that are the chief material of the secondary poets...In fact the medium is common speech and common decasyllabics'. Even though the poetry depended on a cumulative effect and could be rewritten as prose, it was 'poetry because it is better than prose'.[4] Meanwhile, Frost exhorted Thomas to start with his prose style and rewrite it, and to listen to the cadences of everyday language. He particularly drew Thomas's attention to In Pursuit of Spring (1914), with its spare, flowing style, very different from the ornate country writing which Thomas had written at the beginning of his career. These similarities in thought and a recognition of the same mutual path in poetry are the reasons why Thomas was prepared to listen to Frost rather than to the several friends who had also tried to bring out his poetic talent. Besides, Frost was a dominant personality; 'The Golden Room' by Wilfrid Gibson (published in 1927) depicts him holding forth in his New England accent while the circle of Georgian writers listened, entranced:

> In the lamplight
> We talked and laughed; but for the most part, listened
> While Robert Frost kept on and on and on,
> In his slow New England fashion, for our delight...

One man's bore is another man's guru, and although Brooke remained unconvinced by Frost, Thomas was drawn towards the older poet like the proverbial moth to a flame. Yet his poems did not begin until December 1914, a lapse of three months while Thomas no doubt struggled with himself and his destiny in his characteristically clouded way.

The proximity of Abercrombie and Gibson should not be underestimated in this story, for both poets were equally full of plans and capable of demonstrating to Thomas that life as a professional poet was possible. Gibson, convinced that reality and naturalistic speech were the lifeblood of poetry, could have achieved the same outcome as Frost if it was not for the mutual disconnection between himself and Thomas – something fuelled by jealousy as well as mistrust between the Dymock Poets, as Street indicates in *The Dymock Poets* (*DP* 87) and elsewhere. Frost, however, appreciated Gibson's poetry until at least 1914, and the earliest favourable review of *North of Boston* issued not from Thomas, but from Abercrombie, in the *Nation*, 13 June 1914. The situation of these writers in 1914 is therefore one of common goals in criticism and poetry, marred by the unexpected tension generated by new talent and an uncompromising honesty of purpose.[5]

'But I am in it now and no mistake', wrote Thomas to Frost on 15 December 1914, eleven days after writing his first poem, 'Up in the Wind'. He was 'engrossed and conscious of a possible perfection as I never was in prose'. Yet his own style as a poet had to struggle through the mannerisms of Frost at first. In the letter quoted earlier, Thomas queried whether his observation of 'brief unstrained impressions of things lately seen' was 'North of Bostonism'; and when some of Thomas's early poems were shown to W. H. Davies, the latter concluded that they were certainly Frost's work.[6] The biographer Jeffrey Meyers maintains that Thomas was imitating Frost, and if we compare 'Up in the Wind' (*CPET* 3) with a Frost narrative from *North of Boston*, we can see how closely the new poet follows his master.

Thomas records an intense, private drama in 'Up in the Wind', much as Frost does in 'The Death of the Hired Man', a poem he particularly admired. The reader must supply the context to Thomas's narrative poem in the same way as Frost's, for there are no lengthy scene-settings and details to take our attention away from what the characters are saying. Thomas reports naturalistic speech directly, even at the risk of sounding awkward with parentheses and repetitions: 'Came with an engine and a little boy/ (To feed the engine) to cut up timber here' (ll. 55–6). It is all part of the truth and realism he so desired and found in Frost's work. Noticeably, Thomas repeats the leisured tread adopted by Frost so that the poem unfolds gradually, like a story. It has the linear movement of prose without being prosaic as poetry. In the hands of a lesser poet, such material could be merely dull; but Thomas had twenty years of experience as an acute observer of nature and humanity. He automatically knows which incidents will translate across to the reader in the same way that Frost, with his twenty years' worth of unpublished poetry manuscripts, knew too.

Thomas invests 'Up in the Wind' with a dramatic atmosphere – the isolation of the inn, its air of disrepute, its hostile environment, and the 'wild' girl who works there, all contribute to narrative interest. Like Thomas, we want to know why the girl is 'wild', and why the inn is in that location. Such a choice of subject matter may have been influenced by the dramatist in Frost, who was adept at tales with a sinister, even ghoulish undertone; dead babies, skeletons and secretive strangers form part of his stage repertoire in poems like 'Home Burial', 'A Hundred Collars' and 'The Witch of Coos' (the latter poem is in *New Hampshire*, 1923). Both men were 'much acquainted with the night'.

Initially, Thomas followed Frost's advice and rewrote earlier prose passages as the poetry that Frost could see. Sections of *The South Country* (1909), *The Icknield Way* (1913), and *In Pursuit of Spring* (1914) have been detected by critics in subsequent poems. Short works, too, found their origins in prose – 'The Combe', a powerful description of an overgrown hollow, derives from a book review.[7] This helps to account for some of his 'North of Bostonism', that of rendering country incidents into manageable sections of poetry. But Thomas's early method also illustrates that he was unwilling to trust his own instincts as they existed at the point of composition. He is recycling earlier material rather than starting with a clean slate – he is not tempted to begin a poem unless he has the security of prose behind him. It is a pragmatic approach, in sharp contrast to some of his Dymock colleagues, who were content to go 'rhyming on'. Such an attitude would have derived not only from the encouragement of Frost, but from his position as a professional recorder of the landscape, where everything he saw and experienced was a potential quarry for saleable prose.

Fortunately, Thomas does not imitate Frost any more than necessary. In those first few poems written at Steep in December 1914, some of the familiar, introspective Thomas traits announce their presence. He is indecisive, even suicidal: 'At twenty you wished you had never been born' ('The Signpost'), and he gives an unsettling picture of a man with no identity in 'The Other'. He shows his fondness for plants ('Old Man'), his knowledge of folklore, and has an unexpectedly 'modernist' short circuit in phrasing at times: 'The loss of the brook's voice/ Falls like a shadow' ('The Mountain Chapel').

Thomas's development as a poet was hastened in early January 1915 after he sprained his ankle in the hills above Steep, near Petersfield in Hampshire. He was confined to the house for several weeks, and poetry was his main creative outlet – he wrote five more poems between 7 and 9 January, including the ever-popular 'Adlestrop'. This poem, often anthologized, encapsulates Englishness for so many readers that it is often forgotten that Thomas was closer to being a Welshman, born of Welsh parents who had migrated to London.

Due to his enlistment in 1915, Thomas has been included in the roll-call of war poets even though the onset of war plays a small part in his total poetic output. As with Owen and others, we can read a record of his life as a participant in the 1914–18 war disseminated through his letters and published journal extracts, with a good selection of the latter being available in the *Collected Poems* edited by R. George Thomas. But his poetry depends largely on his recording of a soon-vanishing England, seen by us in retrospect, where war is a cloud on the horizon. As an example, see 'As the Team's Head Brass' (*CPET* 108), for his weaving of war issues into a pastoral poem:

> 'Have many gone
> From here?' 'Yes.' 'Many lost?' 'Yes, a good few.
> Only two teams work on the farm this year.
> One of my mates is dead. The second day
> In France they killed him. It was back in March,
> The very night of the blizzard, too. Now if
> He had stayed here we should have moved the tree.'

His ploughman may start 'for the last time' across the field, but only a postwar generation could interpret this as 'for the last time for ever', knowing the analogy of poets and more ploughmen joining the dead labourer mentioned in the extract above. 'This Is No Petty Case of Right or Wrong' (*CPET* 86) and 'A Private' (*CPET* 24) are two rare examples of Thomas as a direct

44

commentator on the arguments of war and the likely result. Yet the Private is described in his habitat at home in England, and Thomas admits his own confusion in 'This Is No Petty Case', relying on his natural patriotism to support him now that he is 'Dinned with war and argument'. The attitude he exhibits is one of unwillingness to be a 'War Poet', and he writes about war issues because they are happening alongside his usual field of reference as a poet.

Thomas's mysticism is mentioned by commentators on his life and works, and it seems that his strong connection with 'otherness' derives from several sources. There is Thomas himself, endlessly searching for his true direction – his 'chronic vacillating habits' as noticed by Frost[8] and his consciousness that whatever route he has chosen, another one would have sufficed just as well. It creates an impression of coexistence and duality, as if the untaken choice is already there, and continually there, beyond the door he did not open and the path he did not take. Then, there is Thomas's physical isolation in many of the poems. He is 'Walking Tom', meeting the farmers, the ploughmen and the barmaids, but he is never one of them. His accent would have signalled 'gentry' to any landworker in Wiltshire or Hampshire in 1915. He may be close to the land in spirit, an 'old inhabitant of earth', but he is unfailingly middle class in his choice of literary occupation. His periodic dejection, too, gave ample time for reflection on otherness – Thomas the mystic is more than half in love with death, and the memento mori effect reappears time after time in the poetry. In 'Lights Out', the first line, 'I have come to the borders of sleep', blurs the distinction between two types of sleep – we do not know initially whether he means the border connecting him with wakefulness, or the permanent sleep of death.

Thomas also writes subject matter which is conventionally mystical, a trait suddenly modern and attractive to readers in a post-orthodox Christian society. He involves figures from legend, such as 'Lob', a hedgerow presence similar to the Green Man, who appears in more places than one and lives through several generations. He is potentially the man talking to Thomas at the end of the poem: 'With this he disappeared/ In hazel and thorn tangled with old man's beard', meaning that the walking poet has been privileged with a glimpse of the other England he seeks. In

'Roads' (*CPET* 88), he envisages the goddesses and Sarn Helen of Welsh legend, the latter fortuitously carrying the same name as his wife, another sturdy walker. The roads of Thomas's poem have presence; they are not flat strips of dirt or asphalt laid across the landscape, but avenues for the living and the dead, overlooked by ancient goddesses and travelled on by spirits. Roads feel, too:

> They are lonely
> While we sleep, lonelier
> For lack of the traveller
> Who is now a dream only.

Landscape, and the figures in it, are symbolic of otherness to such an extent that Thomas himself is sometimes unwittingly trapped. A fully developed example of this occurs in 'The Other' (*CPET* 10), where a semblance of Thomas has already taken the route that the 'real' Thomas is now engaged on. He has a 'doppelganger' and, by the final stanza, we know that Thomas is destined to follow the pursuit until death: 'He goes: I follow: no release/ Until he ceases. Then I also shall cease.' It is as though the person he is pursuing is the real version, an inhabitant of a landscape where the villagers recognize the one ahead, but not the bewildered follower. When he accidentally meets his 'other' in the tenth stanza, the real Thomas is silent, while the semblance asks for him in a reversal of the usual situation; the poet has lost his identity while the double has gained one. Thus, Thomas slips between two worlds, increasingly aware that the 'other' is more significant than himself.

As Thomas writes his otherness into the poetry, it is we, the readers of today, who have access to that perfected version of Thomas on paper, as opposed to the self-negating writer beset by worry and a sense of failure in 1913. His difficulty with location, time, duality and identity helps to perpetuate the image of an enigmatic poet whose affinity with shadows happens in spite of himself. We know, for instance, that the real Thomas had cold baths in the morning and tidied the earth closet in the communal yard at Steep. But Thomas's poetic imagination is 'away, somewhere, away for ever', and it is far stronger than the deadening effect of all those years of hackwork written to order.

Naturally, the new poet set about getting his work into print as soon as the first few poems were completed to his satisfaction. Poems were forwarded to Eleanor Farjeon for typing and commentary, and to Frost for his expert eye. At first, Thomas wanted to use the ancestral surname Marendaz as an alternative to Eastaway, another family name; but Farjeon made the decision on his behalf, settling on the name Edward Eastaway. This strategy was adopted so that the poems would stand up on their own merits, independently of Thomas's reputation as a prose writer. Marsh and Monro declined to include his work in the forthcoming *Georgian Poetry 1916–17* and subsequent anthologies, despite the protestations of de la Mare and John Freeman, but six poems were published privately by the Pear Tree Press in 1916. These were augmented by a substantial selection in *An Annual of New Poetry* (Constable, 1917), where he was represented by eighteen poems, including 'Old Man,' 'Snow', 'The Aspens', and 'Roads'. The collection was edited by Gordon Bottomley and R. C. Trevelyan, and only Abercrombie, sharp as ever, guessed the identity of Eastaway. Five days before Thomas was killed at Arras, he was able to read the *TLS* review sent out by Bottomley, which declared (among some reservations) that Thomas was 'a real poet, with the truth in him'. The vagaries of poetic fame may have had negative consequences for Abercrombie and Gibson, but for Thomas the opposite was the case. After a slow start, his reputation rose inexorably, shaming the shortsightedness of Harold Monro (who also rejected T. S. Eliot) and the political misjudgement of Edward Marsh. Through J. W. Haines in Gloucestershire, the individualistic Georgian poet Ivor Gurney seized on Thomas's *Poems* and *Last Poems* (Selwyn & Blount, 1917 and 1918), becoming one of the first to appreciate this genuine alternative to fragmentary modernist 'isms' in early twentieth-century poetry.

Thomas readily acknowledged Frost as the 'only begetter' of his poetic life, and it seems that the relationship worked both ways, for Frost wrote more than one poem about his British friend, whom he regarded as a brother. One of these poems is 'Iris by Night' (1917), commemorating a walk taken by the two men over the lower slopes of the Malverns in August 1914. In it, Frost describes the phenomenon of a circular rainbow, enclosing them in a natural embrace which seals them 'From all division time or foe can bring', although 'I alone of us have lived to tell'. Frost, who received the news of Thomas's death shortly before writing the poem, seems to be using the rainbow to protect Thomas from his fate as well as recognizing it as a symbol of elected friendship. However, in Frost's landscape, heightened emotions, psychology and 'otherness' combine to create a nebulous impression which leaves the reader wondering what kind of rainbow is happening there. It is Thomas the new poet, utterly sure of himself for once in his life, who had the firmness of touch when writing a dreamlike, potentially nebulous scene, as in 'Wind and Mist' (1915). In this poem, based on a tenancy experienced by the Thomases between 1909 and 1913, he describes the position of a hilltop house:

> But the eye watching from those windows saw,
> Many a day, day after day, mist – mist
> Like chaos surging back – and felt itself
> Alone in all the world, marooned alone.
> We lived in clouds, on a cliff's edge almost
> (You see), and if clouds went, the visible earth
> Lay too far off beneath and like a cloud.
> I did not know it was the earth I loved
> Until I tried to live there in the clouds
> And the earth turned to cloud.[9]

Thomas encapsulated something of his debt to Frost in the mysterious poem 'A Dream' (*CPET* 76), partly based on notebook images and partly on a real dream experienced by the poet. 'I dreamt we were walking near Ledington but we lost one another in a strange place', he wrote to Frost, in July 1915 (*CPET* 150). He is remembering the walks of August 1914, although the force of the water described in the poem is dream imagery, not at all like the tiny streams of south Herefordshire. It is difficult not to interpret the torrent 'running a short course under the sun' as a symbol for the sudden outpouring of poetry unleashed by contact with the sympathetic Frost. The American had led him to the water, but only Thomas himself could take the necessary step and become overwhelmed by it:

> I was bemused, that I forgot my friend
> And neither saw nor sought him till the end,
> When I awoke from waters unto men
> Saying: 'I shall be here some day again'.

4

John Drinkwater
'Those are celestial chimney pots'

John Drinkwater (1882–1937) belongs to the select band of Georgians who did not study at college or university. His formal education ended when he left Oxford High School, meaning that he was self-educated beyond the age of 15. Unlike Brooke, Abercrombie and Thomas, he did not exist from an early age in a milieu of editors, wits and university friends; and he did not spring from a secure middle-class background which he could rebel against with some sense of confidence. Abercrombie, Gibson and Thomas experienced poverty, but they did not start from a position of financial insecurity, the sort which caused Drinkwater senior to encourage his son into the insurance industry in an effort to provide a prosperous future for the young John. As a result, Drinkwater spent many years in an uncongenial office environment, hoping to cross over from this unpromising start to the artistic life he had desired all along. His literary/theatrical life was achieved against great odds, and it was sustained because Drinkwater, more than most other poets, was able to write for a popular market with little sense of compromise. When he abandoned poetic drama for prose drama between 1917 and 1921, it was because he sensibly recognized its theatrical failure in the long term – and his income was related to the economics of supply and demand in the theatre in a way that other Georgians' incomes were not. His pragmatic decisions enabled him to continue as a successful playwright long after the Georgian experiment had petered out, and his willingness to tackle any kind of literary work meant that he could sustain his career as a writer even though his poetry attracted much adverse criticism. Owing to his diverse output, this chapter will concentrate on the poetry and some of the drama until 1922, coinciding with the main period of Georgianism and the availability of comments to assist a contextual setting of the works.

Drinkwater himself is an elusive character, subjected to comments which can easily be interpreted in a negative way. A relevant comment by Catherine Abercrombie has already been quoted in the Introduction (p. 3), but in the original source, not quoted by Street, Catherine Abercrombie goes on to say that Drinkwater became a friend of the family. Nevertheless, the picture generated is one of an irritating 'performer', an image corroborated by reports of him being an 'endlessly willing' reader at Harold Monro's Poetry Bookshop readings. This naturally effusive attitude towards spreading his genius cannot have endeared him to all his listeners, but one must bear in mind that Drinkwater regarded poetry as a high calling, and that performance was one way of presenting himself as a poet as opposed to an insurance officer.

Ambition, and a sense of his own uneasy position as a writer, is doubtless behind Drinkwater's tendency to quibble over minor points raised by other writers in his work. And the same insecurity lies behind his constant generous tributes to the Birmingham impresario Barry Jackson, who rescued him from the insurance industry and enabled his full-time transition to acting and the arts, the work that meant 'joy and liberation'.[1] Drinkwater makes it quite clear that he owed everything to Jackson, and so did the other hopeful amateurs who shared in the same vision of a first-rank theatre for Birmingham: it was 'perhaps the only paradise that could be realised on earth'.[2]

Drinkwater's belief in an artistic earthly paradise helps to set the tone for most of his poetry. He is an idealist, and there is a discrepancy between the life he was leading from day to day, and the life he led in his poetry. In the latter he is a 'dreaming John'; the countryman; in the former, he was a businessman moving through the ranks, with a career change about to take him from drudgery to 'liberation'. It is unfortunate that more of the real life did not get into the poetry, for Drinkwater lived through a period of artistic ferment in his adopted city, and he was at the cutting edge in theatrical circles in the same way that Rutland Boughton and Granville Bantock were in theirs.[3] This divergence between the life and the art helps to illustrate another difference between himself and his Georgian colleagues. In 1913–14, Gibson and Abercrombie appear cottage-bound by comparison, with their adventurings well and truly over, writing reams of poetry in domestic isolation, venturing out occasionally to give readings and meet the publishers. Only Drinkwater was in the thick of things, in close proximity to volatile temperaments, rehearsal schedules, urban noise and demanding audiences. Perhaps because of this, his poetry took on the guise of a second escape route – this time, from the theatre of liberation as opposed to the insurance office. He now lived the artistic life, and therefore his poetry had to become something else, a different kind of escape route. He is consequently more countrified than the country poets, and more open to writing ingenuous lyrics than the naturally open and ingenuous Gibson.

Among the Dymock Poets, his nearest equivalent is Lascelles Abercrombie. Both were idealists, and both seek spiritual references for their poetry; they were passionate about poetic drama, and they admired one another's work. 'The Fires of God' (in *Georgian Poetry 1911–12* and *Poems 1908–14*) shows him at his most Abercrombie-esque in a long poem, adopting the same vatic strain:

> Time gathers to my name;
> Along the ways wheredown my feet have passed
> I see the years with little triumph crowned
> Exulting not for perils dared, downcast...

This poem includes Drinkwater's spiritual journey towards freedom, yet it is hard to disentangle this theme from the attendant generalizations about God, creativity and the world of men. The poet set creativity on such a high pinnacle that only the most ornate and pompously self-aggrandizing phrases would do in a work like this. The same traits mar Abercrombie's longer works, but whereas Abercrombie can rescue his work with village humour and shock tactics, Drinkwater is less capable of variety. In the words of the early critic Mary Sturgeon,[4] he was 'regular with an immobile regularity in which the primal fire was apt to burn low'. It is likely that Drinkwater's activities meant that he spread himself too thinly in his poetry, yet the age abounded in characters who could (and did) push ahead in more than one branch of the arts, following in the tradition of William Morris. The problem with Drinkwater is that his poetry aspires to a position which he cannot reach, and the 'primal fire' burns low as a result. Elsewhere, sections of prose show us that the flame is a strong one:

> I have no sympathy for the writers who, with an active desire for the theatre, refuse to come out and fight the battles of the theatre and learn its lessons, preferring to mumble incompetently in barns and summer-houses, protesting that the theatre has gone to the devil and that they are the only true apostles of light.[5]

Like other first-wave Georgians, Drinkwater was prepared to fight, to take on the artistic mainstream in the pursuit of his art. And such comments tend to be submerged under the general opinion that his verse typified what was undesirable about the Georgian ethos.

As in 1916 when Sturgeon's critical study was published, it is easy for the reader of today to see what is 'wrong' with Drinkwater's verse more than seventy years after it was written. He does not give us any invigorating imagery, makes little attempt at psychological insight, and is concerned with a narrow range of lyrical effects. For these reasons, he does not seem to engage in the pre-First World War scene as a poet in society, and we know little of his inner life as a poet. He has nothing to say to the gimlet-eyed critic, and this is why his verse has proved unattractive to literary historians and those who elucidate the difficult. It gives little beyond the words on the page; it means itself and nothing else; and the poems are the products of a genuinely marketable writer instead of that critical favourite, the unrecognized genius.

Despite his love of the country and the pastoral nature of his verse, Drinkwater was essentially a townie to the end, observing country life through rose-tinted binoculars, squeamish of cowpats and unpicturesque locals, unfamiliar with the rural darknesses where there are no gas lamps. His abortive attempt to sleep under the stars in Abercrombie's garden (DP 68) indicates a nervous temperament unfitted for the realities of country life. He is an observer rather than a participant, and there is a focus on lyricism, innocuous merrymaking, and musing on country ways. The following stanza illustrates the

characteristic subject matter and the consequent 'Eng Lit'
dilemma with a Drinkwater lyric:

> A little land of mellowed ease
> I find beyond my broken gate,
> I hear amid the laden trees
> A magic song, and there elate
> I pass along from sound and sight
> Of men who fret the world away, –
> I gather rich and rare delight
> Where every day is holy day.

('The Broken Gate')[6]

It is formally sound, like so much of Drinkwater's poetry;
nobody could accuse him of being an inept technician. But in
this poem, and elsewhere, there is a concentration on smallness
and picture-frame limitation. He seeks for the spiritual in
everyday occurrences, but his triviality of observation – a pretty
scene resulting in a general uplift – is without any adventur-
ousness or insight. He does not, like Edward Thomas, talk to the
local who might be singing in the above stanza, and he does not
go in search of the elusive 'magic song' like Thomas does in
'The Unknown Bird'. Significantly, Drinkwater is on the outside
of the gate, rather than in among the apple trees – he is no more
part of the scene than he is in 'Mamble', where the poet never
went; in 'Mamble'[7] the opportunity to take 'the road less
travelled by' (in Frost's words) is ignored. Drinkwater's orchard
is altogether too safe and static for readers who are familiar with
Frost's orchards and Thomas's country wanderers, and he is
unwilling to take any risks with his imagination. Drinkwater's
countryside may be as real as Thomas's, but there is less
engagement between the writer and the subject, resulting in
less engagement between the reader and the poem. Drinkwater
is a skilled writer of stanzas rather than a deep thinker and
feeler; rarely a recipe for vivid, memorable lines.

Elsewhere, the poet aims for an effect which he cannot
achieve within the scope of the poem. In 'Elizabeth Ann' (*Tides*,
1916), he has a weak attempt at Masefieldian realism: 'This is the
tale of Elizabeth Ann/ who went away with her fancy man'. We
soon learn that Elizabeth Ann is poor and in a boring job,
working from 'seven to six' polishing candlesticks. She does not
appear to be a happy character, and the reader is more likely to

congratulate her for running away with her fancy man rather than agree with Drinkwater's attitude towards her. His last line, exhorting the wealthy to 'Give her your charity, give her your prayers', is pitched as though she were a Victorian fallen woman like Hardy's 'ruined maid'. Yet none of the preceding lines have justified such a weighty conclusion. An overall impression of bathos is generated by this poem, largely because it leads up to a dramatic final line which throws the bald contents of the rest of the poem into greater relief. The same inadvertent killing of a lyric also occurs in 'Blackbird' (*Loyalties*, 1919/*DPA* 65), concluding with the line 'Those are celestial chimney pots'. Here, Drinkwater again reaches for the poetic and other-worldly, and misses. As a climax to a poem, it is almost comic in its jangling juxtaposition of the ordinary and the celestial, and it is by no means unusual. This is the fifth stanza of 'Dominion',[8] where Drinkwater celebrates summer's bounty:

> And all these things seemed very glad,
> The sun, the flowers, the birds on wing,
> The jolly beasts, the furry-clad
> Fat bees, the fruit, and everything.

Here, unintentional comedy occurs through the sheer banality of the language. No wonder the critics between 1912 and 1921 found it easy to savage his work: 'Mr. Drinkwater's little lyrics of nature and man, sonnets and occasional verses, are not, to speak frankly, of any great importance', wrote the *TLS* critic reviewing *Olton Pools* in 1917. Worst of all, Drinkwater has 'nothing less than a serious misconception of the significance of his contribution to the art' (the *TLS* again, on *Seeds of Time*, 1921). These two comments provide us with a flavour of the criticism levelled at him, although the wider, less intellectual reading public did not necessarily agree. Some critics, too, found his thoughtful English moderation very acceptable during a time of war; *Swords and Ploughshares* (1915) had gone through four reprintings by 1922, while *Poems 1908–1914* achieved six impressions between 1917 and 1922, indicating a certain amount of commercial success.

The innocuous nature of Drinkwater's verse made it acceptable to the public, if not critically favoured. Such works as 'A Town Window' (published in *New Numbers*, *Georgian Poetry*

1913–15, and *Swords and Ploughshares*) unite his best qualities as a poet, combining his attraction to traditional forms, his honest readability, and his lack of pretension when the singing robes were cast aside. It is currently published in the Hart anthology (*DPA* 59), along with other happy, lyrical confections such as 'Mamble' and 'Cotswold Love'. These poems are elegantly written escapism. But when Drinkwater's real-life Birmingham environment imposes on his subject matter to a greater extent, there is a descriptive talent at work with some impetus behind it. It is as though the poet in him could rise to the occasion as a social commentator in the Gibsonian manner when the visual stimulus was effective enough. We can see this in the first stanza of 'In Lady Street', published in *Poems 1908–1914*:

> All day long the traffic goes
> In Lady Street by dingy rows
> Of sloven houses, tattered shops –
> Fried fish, old clothes, and fortune-tellers –
> Tall trams on silver-shining rails,
> With grinding wheels and swaying tops,
> And lorries with their corded bales,
> And screeching cars. 'Buy, buy!' the sellers
> Of rags and bones and sickening meat
> Cry all day long in Lady Street.

Lady Street evidently left an impression on the poet, for he mentions it again in 'Daffodils' (*DPA* 66), where 'You should be borne, if all were well / In golden carts to Lady Street'. The street represents all that is bad in Drinkwater's world – poverty, urbanization, overcrowding – yet paradoxically it enables him to write a poem which struggles to escape from the sterile, perfected mould he imposes on his writing abilities elsewhere. Drinkwater is inclined to shut away scenes that remind him of poverty and inequality, as if his own early struggles were too shameful and hated to be used in his work. If he had felt psychologically able to approach this aspect of himself in his poetry, the amount of externally observed prettiness would have been tempered with the real iron which he must have possessed in his soul.

His verse may have had its limitations, but Drinkwater was an author in the complete sense, with plays, criticism, biography, autobiography and essays to his credit. Above all, he was a professional theatre man, which meant that the inept country poet was far more astute at practical theatre business than his poetic drama colleagues Gibson and Abercrombie, who sound suspiciously like the summer-house mumblers mentioned in the quotation from *Discovery* given earlier. We must therefore look to Drinkwater's theatrical work for the literary strength which eludes us elsewhere. On closer investigation, the poet whose verses compare unfavourably with other Georgians begins to stand out not only as a writer whose frenetic activity generated a commercially successful career, but one whose achievements realized the ambitions which Abercrombie had set for himself, but failed to attain.

Cophetua (1911) was his first published drama, but it is *Rebellion* (1914) which attracts the attention of students of Georgian poetry, for it stood near the beginning of the Georgian drama experiment, and was seen by Marsh, Gibson and Abercrombie in the opening week at Birmingham, on 2 May. The play was published by David Nutt, to coincide with the première: one way in which a writer could increase his income at an opportune moment while audience interest was at its height. *Rebellion* tells the story of a mythical state plunged into civil war by Narros, a former right-hand man to the tyrannical King Phane. The Queen (Shubia) conspires with Narros, but while King Phane is being deposed, she is accidentally killed in 'another part of the field'. Narros consequently loses his will to power, and is driven off to seek his own spiritual salvation while the victorious troops call out his name. It is a study of power, ambition and loss, avoiding the easy moralizing one finds in Drinkwater's poetry collections. The two male protagonists are strong characters, and while the death of Shubia proves unconvincing as an offstage incident, it is nevertheless a believable catalyst for a reversal of fortune and a change in attitude experienced by the rebellious Narros.

In the Bodleian draft of this play, Drinkwater reveals himself as a fluent writer of dialogue. He has few doubts about what his characters are saying, and there are minor changes helping to set the scene with greater accuracy as the picture becomes clearer in his mind. The staging of this play in 1914, overseen by the writer, shows the standards which the Birmingham Repertory staff were aiming for; costumes were influenced by

Bakst, the modish designer to Diaghilev. In 1914 this was striking and up to date.

Abercrombie described the play as 'uncompromising', and comments on the twofold idea of rebellion it encompasses – a physical rebellion against tyranny, and a spiritual rebellion against duty and what the world expects. Furthermore, the conception of the play as *poetic* drama was entirely appropriate: 'Only poetry can plausibly condemn the world's most crucial affairs as no more plausible than "the sound of a broken dish/ Rattled among the scourings of the house" '. Abercrombie goes on to say: 'Mr. Drinkwater's imagery is concrete enough, and lavish; but it is all directed towards a single focus, and as it were lays sensuous emphasis on a metaphysical speculation'.[9] The 'sensuous emphasis' highlights the difference between Drinkwater the playwright and Drinkwater the poet; in the latter incarnation, there is not enough expressed sensuousness written on the page to support the metaphysics.

Drinkwater's next play, *The Storm* (1915), proved to be a popular one-act drama, described as 'lucky in performance' by its author. Its first performance was on 8 May, with a subsequent run in Stratford-on-Avon during August, and revivals at Birmingham in 1916 and 1918. As in *Rebellion*, it laid heavy demands on the principal actor, something acknowledged by the author in his preface to the published edition in 1917. Drinkwater imagined a combination of 'emotional grip' and 'nervous energy' in the part of Alice, and it is a dominant part, providing a great opportunity for an actress with 'staying power'. In this play, we can see the Georgian recognition of strong female characters given some substance; Alice is troubled, but she is not a schemer or a crone like the dismal women of *King Lear's Wife*. *The Storm* is a short play (eighteen pages), and it follows the emotional changes of Alice as she awaits news of her husband, lost on the hills in the eponymous storm. She is accompanied by two women, who supply a commentary on her condition while providing the support and realism she needs in order to survive the ordeal. We know by the end of the play that her husband is dead, something realized earlier by Sarah, the elder of the group. The play is therefore a portrayal of an extreme state of mind, rather than a tragedy in the usual sense of death and disaster happening during the course of the action to characters who start from a position of stability. In order that the events onstage should not be confined to a closed circle, we are provided with an opposing point of view by way of contrast; a young traveller enters near the end of the play, exulting in the storm and its effects. In Brooke's *Lithuania*, a similar young intruder neither helps nor throws any light on the tragedy he has stumbled into. In Drinkwater's *Storm*, the excitable intruder, with his ability to survive the storm and enjoy it, serves to show up the claustrophobic atmosphere being generated by the waiting women, and the suspicion that their fears might be unfounded.

The Birmingham audience received Drinkwater's play warmly (not a reaction associated with Brooke's *Lithuania* – see chapter 5) and a subsequent review in the *Birmingham Post* praises the author for his 'fine imagery', claiming that the work 'deserves alike the loyalty of the actors and the cordiality of the audience'. Above all, *The Storm* 'counts among Mr. Drinkwater's best work', and it is described as 'a poignant and penetrating study of a woman's anguish'.

His poetry makes little reference to events in Europe during 1914–18, but this is not to discredit it. As the Ross *Georgian Revolt* explains, many minor poets undertook to write war verse, with corresponding clever satires from the modernists and critics. It is a mark of Drinkwater's integrity that he stuck to what he knew and did it well; his sealed-off Georgian time capsule survived the war intact, and he continued as a poet long after some 'war poets' had experienced a reversal of style. As an example of the latter, see Robert Nichols, whose expressionistic 'The Assault'[10] belies the fact that his main output consisted of poems with titles like 'A Faun's Holiday'.

Drinkwater's remaining poetic drama bears out the theory that he placed more intellectual energy and social commitment in his theatre works. *The God of Quiet* (1916) takes place outside a war-torn city, beside the statue of a peace-loving god. This statue is destroyed by one of the warlords, whereupon the statue speaks the fateful words: 'Not one of you in all the world to know me'. The symbolism of the play is obvious, and Drinkwater drives home his pacifist message by repeating similar words in the concluding line of the play, spoken by a beggar instead of the god: 'Not one of us in all the world to know you'. Peace is destroyed, and 'the noise of arms break[s] out again as the curtain falls'. The war in the play, like the war in Flanders, is an ongoing process.

The God of Quiet is a symbolic and didactic piece, but the succeeding play, $X = 0$ (1917), is linear and explanatory, and just as effective in its pacifist message. According to Abercrombie, it was the most successful of the one-act plays. Drinkwater's unusual title, often the first marketing device a play can possess, refers to the equation demonstrated in the text. Opposing Greeks and Trojans, at war over Helen of Troy, cancel each other out, and two of the main players are dead at the end of the act. We learn of the hopes and dreams of both sides during the short scenes, realizing that neither of them wishes to be involved in the war. While they sit and wait for action, their real lives are being wasted and their talents unused. Moreover, the Greeks think of home:

> PRONAX   It's a dear home,
> And fragrant, and there's blessed fruit and corn
> And thoughts that make me older than my youth
> Come even from the nettles at the gate.
> Today, perhaps, the harvesters are out
> And on the night is the ripe pollen blown...
> And this is the third harvest that has gone
> While we are wasted on a barren plain
> To avenge some wrong done in our babyhood
> On beauty that we have not seen.

In this extract, the Greek's homesickness for his home territory is poignantly conveyed by his attachment to the common nettles as well as the fruit and corn. 'How should we hate the dead?' replies Salvius later:

> And, where death ranges, as among us now,
> You, Pronax, I, and our antagonists
> And friends alike are all but as dead men
> Moving together in a ghostly world...

In 1918, the war poets had reached much the same conclusion as Salvius: see Wilfred Owen's 'Strange Meeting', where a projection of Owen meets his comradely German in the non-world of death. 'I am the enemy you killed, my friend'. In $X = 0$, Pronax has enough time to reflect on the horror of killing a young Trojan (scene 3) before discovering that his friend Salvius has been murdered by a Trojan in his absence. The play is simple and powerful, and its blank verse moves with naturalistic ease in comparison with the deliberate poetic mannerisms found in *The God of Quiet*.

During 1917–18, Drinkwater experienced a change of mind regarding poetic drama. There are several reasons why this should occur at such a date. Drinkwater had written five successful ones for the Birmingham theatre, and the management prided itself on its ambitious programme – yet the war years had taken their toll, and the standby repertoire of Shakespeare, Shaw and Galsworthy was becoming predictable. It would take more than another one-act play to revive the fortunes of the company. Furthermore, Drinkwater was in a good position to see the future of an art-form which was at best rarefied beyond the great Elizabethan age. Abercrombie the theorist was never a practical stage manager, and he did not depend on theatre receipts for the continuance of his career. As he states in the Drinkwater memorial lecture of 1937, he was obsessed with what the theatre *should* be (the position of a dreamer), whereas Drinkwater was more concerned with what it *could* be; putting the dream into practice. Economic factors may have influenced Drinkwater into giving up writing drama which used poetic language, but the seeds were already sown in $X = 0$, where the language has a greater flexibility due to its closeness to ordinary speech. On a personal level, Drinkwater in late 1917 stood on the cusp between moderate success as a writer/director and potential fame – it would take something on a grander scale than $X = 0$ to propel him into lasting fame as a playwright, and he would lose nothing by changing his style.

Abraham Lincoln (1918) could not be more different from $X = 0$. It has a large cast, not including the walk-on parts of assorted ladies and gentlemen, two Chroniclers, an optional orchestra, and settings which give scope for elaborate stage-design. The play has a five-year historical span, starting with Lincoln's acceptance of the presidency in 1860, and concluding with his assassination in 1865. It is a history play in the traditional sense, as though Drinkwater was attempting to do for his subject matter what Shakespeare had achieved on behalf of the Tudor dynasty. And it was wildly successful. The published version alone ran to thirteen impressions between October 1918 and mid-1921, and its elevation of the plain American virtues of straight talking and liberty meant that it played to enthusiastic audiences in the United States. Drinkwater had arrived; he became 'famous in two hemispheres' (Abercrombie) and he never looked back.

The play succeeds on several levels, despite the presence of the Chroniclers, who comment on the action at opportune moments when the scenery is being changed. To the contemporary eye, these figures can seem ponderous and misplaced, but they are the vestiges of Drinkwater's belief that drama can be conveyed through the medium of poetry. The Chroniclers also highlight the artificial nature of the whole affair, that this is a pretence at actuality and an interpretation of historic events. Drinkwater was always quick to cover himself against the charge of inaccuracy in his work, and he states in his prefatory note to the published edition that his attitude is one of the dramatist rather than the historian.

Abraham Lincoln is an exposition of humanitarianism seen against a background of the American Civil War. It is made clear in the play that Lincoln was not a vengeful president, but someone who resorted to war in order to preserve the Union and abolish slavery. We see Lincoln and his invincible wife moving from small-town success to the White House, with Lincoln himself becoming idolized as 'old Abe' and 'Father Abraham', a president armed only with his native wit and the determination to do the right thing. Drinkwater explores issues of hypocrisy and bigotry in a non-threatening way, through the agency of a dialogue between egalitarian Mrs Otherly and the anti-Southern Mrs Blow, the latter being chided by Lincoln for her uncharitable opinions: 'The world is larger than your heart, Madame'.[11] People are seen to humour Lincoln, yet we are left in no doubt, like the characters on stage, that he is the man in charge:

> Seward, you may think I'm simple, but I can see your mind working as plainly as you might see the innards of a clock. You can bring great gifts to this government, with your zeal, and your administrative experience, and your love of men. Don't spoil it by thinking I've got a dull brain.[12]

Drinkwater is representing a complex man, at once approachable and homespun, yet judgemental, incisive and in command. The author has assimilated his sources, turning dry history into a fast-paced believable text with humane characters.

There is an element of pageantry in the play, particularly during the last scene, where the President is assassinated: 'Now he belongs to the ages', intones Stanton, one of his ministers, as soon as the deed is done. Yet the play has a traditionally well-drawn group of main characters, from Lincoln himself to the flustered maid Susan – almost one of the family, but not quite – who is incapable of calling Lincoln 'the President' after years of addressing him as 'Mr Lincoln'. The play appeals to common-denominator factors in the audience; we all wish to see the good people triumph and the evil-doers cast away. Yet Lincoln is a flawed hero in the classical mould, with his untidiness and procrastination, dependent in his youth on the decision-making ability of his wife. He is not perfect, any more than the successful General Grant is superior to General Lee; we do not have simplifications in the play, although the historical plot is made simple for our benefit. Drinkwater hides his subtlety under a wide audience appeal and a potential for spectacle. Nothing could be more different from the closed, hermetic world of the poetic dramas; Drinkwater explodes onto the commercial stage like a man let out of prison.

After overseeing a successful transition of *Lincoln* from Birmingham to London and then to the United States, Drinkwater returned to the British stage with his new play, *Mary Stuart* (1921). In choosing another figure whose personality attracts legend and speculation, the playwright had decided to continue his populist approach. Most people with a grasp of British history have heard of Mary, the doomed cousin of Elizabeth I. She presents a fine opportunity for an actress, and she was already a literary icon thanks to Schiller and (more recently) John Masefield. A revival of the play at Birmingham in 1923 shows the mixed reaction of the *Birmingham Post* critic, one which reflects what the reader finds in the published text. It is 'an example of able, earnest, persuasive dramatic advocacy', but the critic was on the whole puzzled by the 'curious introduction' and by the reaction of Mary to Riccio's death. The critic imagined that it was the 'fey' performance of Gwen Ffrancon-

Davies in the lead role, but we can see from the text that Drinkwater envisaged Mary's reaction to be an offhand, distanced one: 'A fantastic nothing...'[13] to preserve her safety in the proximity of an unbalanced husband. In the context of the play, she cannot be seen as Riccio's protector.

Mary Stuart includes the murders of Riccio and Darnley, but the play is centred on Mary herself and the human dilemma of being a queen. She is a person with powerful emotions, yet she is trapped in a powerless position, subjected to intrigue and the suits of unworthy men. Bothwell is ostensibly her rescuer at the end of the play, but we know from Scottish history that he too will join the list of doomed associates. The character of Mary is conveyed largely through cryptic statements, as though she is on an intellectual plane above that of her court:

> MARY No subjects. Only strangers at the table.
> RICCIO I do not understand you, Mary.
> MARY You have said it.
> RICCIO I give you myself, all my poet's heart. Is it not enough?
> MARY You are neither subject nor lord. There is no peace in you, David. Just a buzzing in the jar.[14]

Such exchanges can exaggerate any 'fey' tendency in performance, but they emphasize Mary's dissociation from her court and give her an air of elevation and intelligence. Meanwhile, the three suitors are written with contrast in mind; Riccio the egregious secretary, Bothwell the masculine hero, and Darnley the irrational, jealous husband. It is a measure of Mary's separation that her husband is referred to as Darnley by the playwright and the cast, though he is really Henry Stuart, King of Scotland. This puzzled the *Post* critic in 1923. Contrasting characters, like those expressed by Mary's suitors, help greatly with the transmission of her dilemmas in love. She desires an overwhelming passion equal to her status as queen, but is faced with a *range* of less impressive personalities and court intrigues. When Darnley is dispatched by a gunpowder plot, Bothwell appears as her champion, but we suspect that the trap will tighten around the Queen as another ambitious man claws his way to the top: 'Tomorrow you can proclaim me leader of your arms'.[15] The play is open-ended, dependent on our knowledge of Mary's fate to supply the conclusion.

Drinkwater could have written a straightforward historic

drama, but he chose to include another 'Brechtian' framing device, that of a dialogue between a man with a troublesome relationship in 1900 and an older adviser who bids him remember the history of their Scottish queen. As with the Chroniclers in *Abraham Lincoln*, these intermediaries between the audience and the players are apt to strike the onlooker as unnecessary; we do not need to know about the marital difficulties of John Hunter to understand the play or empathize with the Queen, and we do not need the apparition and clairvoyant dream of the Queen[16] to link the various levels of the play. It takes a far more original modernist than John Drinkwater to juggle with timescales and notions of history in this way, reminding the audience that the foundation of his art is one of solid competence rather than any ability to crash through barriers and 'make it new'.

The pattern of Drinkwater's playwriting career was now set. *Mary Stuart* was followed by *Oliver Cromwell* (also 1921), *Robert E. Lee* (1923), and *Robert Burns* (1925), besides social comedies such as *Bird in Hand* (1927). His poetry and drama continued on parallel paths, and he never again attempted the poetic drama which he had fought to realize with his colleagues during the Georgian years. 'Let us be modern by all means, he seemed to say – but not too modern' (*GR* 86).

5

Rupert Brooke
'Come and die. It'll be great fun'

A young Apollo, golden haired,
Stands dreaming on the verge of strife,
Magnificently unprepared,
For the long littleness of life.

This well-known quotation by Frances Cornford (1886–1960) helped to perpetuate the image of Brooke as an ineffectual 'beautiful' poet, writing his naïve war poetry before going to his own death and being resurrected as a hero. Yet the quotation above could easily refer to the opposite of ineffectuality; a determined and highly motivated character who was 'magnificently unprepared' for a life which promised to be harder and more frustrating than he had originally imagined. Biographical material has revealed Brooke as an achiever by nature, the sort who was regarded as an intellectual and a leader by his associates. He won a fellowship to King's College, Cambridge (1913), and took over his father's responsibilities as a housemaster at Rugby when he was only 22. It is not easy to control fifty privileged boys, yet Rupert Brooke – not quite from the same social class as his charges – managed this difficult task for two months. He was active as a supporter of Cambridge drama, a favoured protégé of Edward Marsh, and a friend of pioneer free-thinkers and modernists such as Virginia Woolf. He was also political to a far greater extent than his Georgian colleagues, so that the mosquito bite in 1915 killed a paid-up member of the Fabian socialist movement as well as a poet.

His famed attractiveness has stood in the way of an unbiased appreciation of the poetry, yet even his photogenic good looks were short-lived and something of an illusion. Childhood photographs show a plump, unprepossessing boy, while later military pictures show a hard, determined expression redolent of the typical young officer. Brooke was adept at fitting into the role expected of him; compare the 'poet' images taken by Sherrill Schell in 1913 with the Royal Naval Division photograph provided in the Hassall biography opposite page 512.

On the surface, Brooke was stylish, entertaining, and a publicist's dream. He magnified his appeal by associating with those whose approval naturally brought him into contact with movers and shakers in the arts and political worlds. He was not prepared for littleness, but for greatness. However, his multifaceted social abilities left him in a directionless state of mind.

> And your California plan is just that, just putting off the real beginning to work at something – you don't really care about orange picking or whatever it is out there, and the longer you put it off the worse it will be to begin, and you will just be wasted...[1]

This exasperated comment from his friend Rosalind Murray shows some of the reality behind the image. Enlisting in the war effort in 1914 would solve this ongoing crisis of waiting, as well as his relationship crises with Ka Cox and others.

Brooke has suffered at the hands of his literary guardians in the past; for example, no full-length biography was allowed until Christopher Hassall took the job upon himself. Although the result can hardly be improved upon, Hassall glossed over several aspects of Brooke's life, and did not have much access to private papers held by Noel Olivier[2] and others. Earlier, Mrs Brooke had impaired Edward Marsh's attempts at writing *Rupert Brooke: A Memoir*, published by Sidgwick & Jackson in 1918. A complete picture did not emerge until the 1970s and thereafter, when it was no longer considered necessary to protect and cover. This illustrates how easy it is for literary guardians to control the public perception of their charges – a phenomenon by no means confined to Brooke's case and frequently with less benevolent intent.[3]

The 'unknown' Brooke is now in the public arena, excavated and documented by several scholars, such as Timothy Rogers in *Rupert Brooke: A Reappraisal and Selection* (1971), where a handy compendium of letters, drama and criticism adds substance to the relatively small output of the poetry. Brooke was a prized correspondent, and the bulk of his entertaining letters make good reading, whatever doubts one may have about his attitude towards lovers, other nations, and the inherent theatricality of his persona. They also provide insight into his developing aims as a writer, particularly in his exchanges with Sidgwick & Jackson's Frank Sidgwick about 'Lust', retitled 'Libido' in *Poems 1911*. And no survey of the lesser-known Brooke would be complete without mentioning his talent as a comedian – observable in his 'Entry of John Rump into Heaven',[4] where his rigid English Gentleman, who stands for 'bijou-residences/Semi-detached' (like Brooke's own 24 Bilton Road, Rugby), routs Heaven and puts even God in the shade. Brooke is against the John Rumps of the world and makes him a figure of fun, yet Rump is a symbol of the materialistic middle class, blotting out the landscape as he grows. He is something to be feared, yet he is the cause of laughter; Brooke's duality is observable even in this occasional piece.

Brooke's first collection was published in 1911, but he had started on his journey as a poet from the age of 10, according to Rogers. There are published works dating from 1903 in the Keynes edition, written when the poet was 16. As Keynes indicates in his preface, the first collection represented seven years' worth of work – a long journey towards a literary life, particularly when this output is compared with the facility displayed by Gibson and Drinkwater. The latter was capable of bringing out one book per year besides working as an actor-manager.

Brooke's influences during 1903–7 were, as Keynes suggests, the 1890s: Wilde, Dowson, Rossetti and Swinburne. His poetry contained lines such as 'the light/ Drooped like a weary lily o'er the sea' and:

> Go, heart, and pluck beside the Path of Dreams,
> Where moans the wind along the shadowy streams,
> Sad garlands wreathed of the red mournful Roses
>   And lilies o'moon beams.

('The Path of Dreams', *PWRB* 194)

The image Brooke presents is that of the pale youth sorrowing, invariably alone and burdened with thoughts of lost love, death and weariness. Apart from the Aesthetic ornamentation in the example quoted above, there is also conventional poetic language ('thou hadst not'), helping to place Brooke in a context of literariness and attitudinizing that was far older than his 17-year-old self. Ironically, Brooke was to experience the real effects of death and loss shortly after these poems were written, when his older brother Richard died in 1907 and his put-upon father died in 1909. Another early influence was Browning, apparently the first poet that Brooke came across (*RB* 28), recognizable later in an associative way from phrases such as 'the first clean rapture'[5] and in some of Brooke's abrupt, colloquial addresses: 'Sir, since the last Elizabethan died' (*PWRB* 87).

Underneath these echoes, the real personality of Brooke the poet struggles to assert itself. It is not only a desire to learn the art which makes him model his work on the 1890s, but his genuine flair for theatricality and pose. He is naturally drawn towards an era when the Artist looked and behaved like one. There were alternative models by 1905, including Housman, whose homoerotic and classical bias might be considered a compatible source of influence. Brooke knew of Housman's work, but did not rate it as highly as Dowson's. In his Rugby final term paper on modern poetry (*RB* 92–5), he is patronizing towards Housman for inclining 'towards doggerel', but he praises Dowson for his 'faint exquisite words', in which he finds 'refuge' from the boom and rant of major poets. This early attachment to a Burne-Jones style in verse was a genuine preference, rather than that of a newcomer aping established models – he valued the older generation of poets and wished to perpetuate their qualities in his early poems.

At the same time, there is much in the early poems showing us what Brooke's eventual achievement was destined to be. The 1903–5 works are juvenilia in that they are not as interesting as his later poems and show the hand of an apprentice. But in 'God Give' (*PWRB* 200) he depicts the plight of a lover who tries to forget his beloved, yet who still wishes to see her. Among the archaisms, he writes 'The tremulous eyelids of my old delight', the sort of ambivalent line one could find in a later poem, where love is being satirized or praised rather than being the subject of vague sentiment. Without the Aesthetic echoes, this poem has a focus on physical attraction wholly characteristic of the later work. In 1903, it is also evident that Brooke has a command over his rhyme schemes.

Religion is an early concern for Brooke, and on balance he favours pagan Earth and Sun alternatives as exemplified by the pre-Christian world. In his sonnet 'The Earth' (*PWRB* 197), Brooke describes 'Our Mother the Earth' as being in a state of pain due to the 'strife' heaped upon her by men:

> from the earth is fled
> The first clean rapture of her primal life.
> She is sore grieved; laden with men's strife
> Woe of the living – burden of the dead.

Lines describing the Earth Mother sit uncomfortably with an appeal to the orthodox Christian God in the penultimate line:

> 'Let me not see anew the cold grey light
> Merciful God – nor feel the dawn again'.
> But still there came no answer to the cry.

This 1904 poem acknowledges alternative world views, and can be understood in the light of late twentieth-century 'new age' ideas, where the earth is a holistic organism capable of hitting back at the mistreatment she suffers. The older Brooke, who later lived with Taatamata and admired the Tahitian freedom from dour work ethic and hypocrisy, experienced first-hand knowledge of a society based on non-Christian religious values.

Brooke's interest in ancient ways of worship materializes again in 'On the Death of Smet-Smet, the Hippopotamus Goddess' (1908), where a tribe of Egyptians pay tribute to their 'Mother', a dual figure who ruled them in fear, but who nevertheless gave them life and protected them. Elsewhere, Brooke writes of 'my Lord the Sun' ('In Examination', *PWRB* 154), who turns a room full of scribbling boys into haloed gods – with the poet confusing the pagan idea of an Apollonian sun god with the more regular Christian vision of angels granted to him towards the end of the poem. It does not suggest a religious divide in Brooke so much as experiment and adventurousness. He knows, from his classical studies, that history is not Anglican. And his natural bias seems to be towards the heroic age where mortals could associate with gods, or at least feel closer to them. Later, the identification with classical mores became dangerously mixed with reality: 'I want to mix a few sacred and Apollonian English ashes with theirs [dead French writers'], lest England be shamed' (*RB* 481).

69

In comparison, the Christian version of God does not stand up to Brooke's expectations. In 'Failure' (1908), he begins: 'Because God put His adamantine fate/ Between my sullen heart and its desires...' and he finds that no God exists when he enters 'the dusty council halls' to make his poet's complaint. Earlier, in 'Song of the Children in Heaven' (1907, *PWRB* 156), the picture is one of restriction and unhappiness, despite the lightness of the verse:

> And when a baby laughs up here
> Or rolls his crown about in play,
> There is a pause. God looks severe;
> The angels frown, and sigh and pray
> And someone takes the crown away.

The state religion of England is anti-play, distanced, closed and frigid in these references, whereas the pagan alternative promises vigour, love, and the natural cycle of birth and death. It is no accident that the Apollonian figure of Brooke became his own Menelaus and went to the wars; his imagination had fitted him for the process long ago.

Later poems bear out this interest in other religions, whether the intention is satirical or not. He continues to refer to the classical world ('The Goddess in the Wood'), depicts an imaginary fish god in 'Heaven' (1913), and eventually finds his own heaven on earth in 'Tiare Tahiti' (1914). Wherever God and Heaven are, they are not something to aspire to in the Christian sense. His famous lines from 'The Soldier', with its 'hearts at peace, under an English heaven', appear to speak to the country churchyardist in all moderate Anglican readers, yet Brooke is celebrating life, not death, in this poem. In particular he is giving back his body to the ground, rather than to God – and as if to reinforce the point, he envisages the soldier/himself becoming a 'pulse in the eternal mind' rather than a harp-wielding angel in a long shirt.

Poems 1911 attracted mixed reviews, interesting for their divergence from the image of the sentimental English patriot generated by the posthumous popularity of 'Grantchester' (1912) and the war sonnets. Brooke was accused of bad taste: 'his disgusting sonnet on love and seasickness ought never to have been printed' (*TLS*, 29 August 1912). This refers to 'A Channel Passage', with its 'emetic' lines:

> Do I forget you? Retchings twist and tie me,
> Old meat, good meals, brown gobbets, up I throw.
> Do I remember? Acrid return and slimy,
> The sobs and slobber of a last year's woe.

'Disgusting' is the general verdict on this poem, yet the critics did not leave it at that. It was described as 'a satiric masterpiece' by the *English Review* (February 1912), and on the whole the poem was seen as an expression of ebullience and youth. Brooke wrote like this because he was young and daring, not because he was a bad poet with nothing to say. The *Saturday Review* of 24 April 1912 recognized Brooke's talent in the collection: 'He varies his manner of attack like a virtuoso upon a musical instrument', but the 'Choriambics' are criticized for seeming to have been written 'for a wager'. He is described as a 'pugnacious' poet (*Nation*, 16 July 1912), and, despite the formal skill acknowledged by several reviewers, he is regarded as a deliberate shocker, an 'épater la bourgeoisie' poet. The combination of frankness and performance is symptomatic of the man, but in 1911–12 it was uncharacteristic of 'minor' poetry. 'A Channel Passage', 'Menelaus and Helen' and 'On the Death of Smet-Smet...' are mentioned most frequently in the 1912 reviews, showing a certain consistency between those poems regarded by the critics as noteworthy.

In 'Menelaus and Helen', Brooke contrasts the romantic legend with the later reality. Poets have written about the 'perfect Knight before the perfect Queen', but what happened next? Brooke the classicist and modernist sets out to tell us:

> white Helen bears
> Child on legitimate child, becomes a scold,
> Haggard with virtue. Menelaus bold
> Waxed garrulous, and sacked a hundred Troys
> 'Twixt noon and supper. And her golden voice
> Got shrill as he grew deafer. And both were old.

Helen becomes a nagging housewife, and Menelaus is a bore. This is what happens to heroes who don't 'die in their glory and never grow old', as Housman writes. Among many other poems, 'Menelaus and Helen' is expressive of Brooke's youth-cult. Age brings no benefits, and even heroes cannot escape time.

In common with other new poets, including Abercrombie and

Frost, Brooke was subjected to the critical eye of Edward Thomas, who reviewed *Poems 1911* in the *Daily Chronicle* of 9 April 1912. Thomas, who knew Brooke and met him several times, recognized what Brooke might be underneath the self-conscious image-making. And in the curious penultimate sentence quoted below, Thomas gives himself away too. He was 35 at the time, with his own youthful revolt long past and only five more years to live.

> He reveals chiefly what he desires to be and to be thought. Now and then he gives himself away, as when in three poems close together, he speaks of the scent of warm clover. Copies should be bought by everyone over forty who has never been under forty. It will be a revelation. Also if they live yet a little longer they may see Mr. Rupert Brooke a poet. He will not be a little one.

Again, Thomas has focused on Brooke's age and his predilection for the passions of youth; and that he will be a poet in the future rather than at the present time of 1912. Reviewers, even those like Thomas with an eye for potential, regard him as a promising poet rather than a smoothly accomplished one. He was a puzzle, rather than a great or a bad poet – an observation expressed again in 1914, when four sonnets in *New Numbers* were described as the result of 'a curiously complex consciousness' (*TLS*, 19 March 1914).

Donne and Browning are Brooke's noticeable influences in 1911 and thereafter, as Brooke himself acknowledged (*RB* 372, 536). They were a contributory factor to the 'insolence' reported by critics. Donne was an early enthusiasm of Brooke's, and it is easy to see why. Metaphysical cleverness, contorted comparisons and energetic love poetry are part of both poets' work, with Brooke mirroring the confident Metaphysical style in poems such as 'Thoughts on the Shape of the Human Body'. Here and elsewhere, the substitution of seventeenth-century spelling would create a convincing pastiche. Brooke has captured the sound and movement of a Metaphysical poem as well as the vocabulary:

> No perfection grows
> 'Twixt leg, and arm, elbow, and ear, and nose
> And joint, and socket; but unsatisfied
> Sprawling desires, shapeless, perverse, denied.

Brooke used his Metaphysical style freely, eventually combining his interest in abstraction and the tomb with the more relaxed environment of Tahiti:

> And you'll no longer swing and sway
> Divinely down the scented shade,
> Where feet to Ambulation fade
> And moons are lost in endless Day.
> How shall we wind these wreaths of ours
> When there are neither heads nor flowers?

('Tiare Tahiti', 1914, *PWRB* 25)

Critics informed of new trends in poetry were quick to spot the Metaphysician in Brooke: 'he would have met with readier appreciation in the seventeenth century' (*Nation*, 8 March 1913). A historicist influence is at the forefront in 'The Funeral of Youth: A Threnody', too, although the mannerisms are closer to a learned eighteenth-century poet, as befitting the subject:

> Round the raw grave they stay'd. Old *Wisdom* read
> In mumbling tone the Service for the Dead.
> There stood *Romance*,
> The furrowing tears had mark'd her rouged cheek,
> Poor old *Conceit*, his wonder unassuag'd;
> Dead *Innocency's* daughter, *Ignorance*;
> And shabby, ill-dress'd *Generosity*.

By 1913, Brooke was a master of voices, able to impersonate any form of poetry dictated by his interests. He had already put this talent to good use at Rugby, writing school competition entries in a consciously weighty style – see 'The Bastille' and 'The Pyramids' (*PWRB* 174, 189).

Brooke's modernism as a poet is most apparent in his works about male–female relationships. Once his Aesthetic period of fainting, insubstantial, literary love had passed, he was an analyst of dilemmas and reactions. In real life his love affairs never ran as expected, and when he quarried his own experience as a lover with a difficult partner, he became an original love poet with something worth saying. He is unafraid of outlining the strong emotions generated by troublesome relationships, including triumph and satisfaction in the notorious 'Lust', which unites the idea of pursuit, sex and death in a Petrarchan sonnet. As if to reinforce the last line,

'Quieter than a dead man on a bed', the Kings College manuscript for this poem has a drawing of a figure on a bier below it. More often, his encounters are not a success. The beloved does not return his interest or understand his thoughts, or may be thinking very differently along less positive lines; see 'The Hill', ending 'And then you suddenly cried and turned away', for an unexpected conclusion to an initially hopeful scene. Brooke is frequently bewildered: 'Myself should I have slain? Or that foul you?' ('Success'), and he does not relish the prospect of growing old with his chosen partner, when 'infinite hungers leap no more/ In the chance swaying of your dress/ And love has changed to kindliness' ('Kindliness'). Everyday married life is a cause for scorn ('Sonnet Reversed'), while anyone insensitive enough to marry someone else in preference to him is a target for invective ('Jealousy'). Brooke ranges from the subtle to the hysterical, giving the reader a roller-coaster of human emotions. It is possible to describe such work as the product of a protracted adolescence, but this would deny Brooke his skilfulness as a writer and his daring in terms of his subject matter. He depicts corrosive human relationships as though they are happening at the present time; not a subject preference one associates with his first-wave Georgian colleagues.

1914 and Other Poems (published in June 1915) consolidated his reputation as a hero/poet, particularly with the five '1914' war sonnets and the irony of the poet's death in April. But this volume also contains his South Seas poetry, showing a relaxed, less 'officer class' Brooke, and fewer love poems involving a shrill, castigating tone. It is as though Brooke had unloaded his anxiety and urgency in *Poems 1911*, and was trading on the residue of the same problems in 1914. He is no longer trying to shock, as the earlier critics had claimed, but some of his characteristic situations return in a less fierce and immediate way. He becomes conventionally lyrical ('Doubts', 'Fafaia'), while, in 'The Great Lover', his depiction of things he has loved includes a catalogue of what can only be described as safe, pretty things – rainbows and flowers – and bourgeois comforts like hot water and clean plates. He experiences the same disappointment in love, but now he expresses the disappointment as opposed to the confusion and jealousy:

> ...But they know, love grows colder
> Grows false and dull, that was sweet lies at most.
> Astonishment is no more in hand and shoulder
> But darkens, and dies out from kiss to kiss.
> All this is love; and all love is but this.

('Love', 1913)

The conqueror image and that of the lively young man have largely disappeared. He is beset by impervious women – 'But heart, she will not care' ('Unfortunate') – and expects to have to compromise instead: 'And I daresay she will do' ('The Chilterns').

Previous pages have mentioned Brooke's ability as a role player in poetry, adopting or presenting a pose. In 1914, after Brooke had experienced a long period of aimless existence, the role of Public Poet asserted itself. 'Now God be thanked Who has matched us with His hour,/ And caught our youth, and wakened us from sleeping'. This sonnet, entitled 'Peace', is the first of his numbered war sonnets.[6] It is the outbreak of war, with death seen as both enemy and friend, which provides the release desired by the poet, and results in the inner peace represented by the title. The protagonist is clearly Brooke, since we know his attitude to love, death and heroism from *Poems 1911* and his letters, yet Brooke turns this sonnet into a public poem by including 'us', 'our', and 'we'. He is speaking on behalf of his generation, the thousands of men comprising the 'we' in 1914 who eagerly rushed to join the war effort, expecting it to be over by Christmas. In the fifth sonnet ('The Soldier', originally entitled 'The Recruit'), Brooke goes even further, citing himself as the representative Englishman. Now he is speaking on behalf of his race, not just as one of their number; 'England' and 'English' are mentioned six times within fourteen lines:

> A body of England's, breathing English air,
> Washed by the rivers, blessed by suns of home.

In this poem, he is the sacrifice on behalf of his nation, made all the more convincing by the ritualistic washing and blessing, and the distancing from real life. He was not born of Mary Ruth Cotterill and William Parker Brooke, but fashioned from the 'dust of England', like a clay idol.

More importantly for literary manuscript history, it seems that

Wilfrid Gibson, the editor of *New Numbers* no. 4 had requested the change of title (*DPA* 71). If the original title of 'The Recruit' had been retained, the emphasis of the poem would be slightly different, with the soldier's naïvety entirely excusable. In real life, Brooke had experienced the effects of battle when he was posted to Antwerp in October 1914. It is symptomatic of his 'complicated consciousness' that he would retread the path of a new recruit in his imagination, putting himself in the lordly sacrificial role, when he had already experienced battle and survived in a plebeian, unglamorous way. By changing the title, Gibson over-simplified his friend's intentions and undermined a poem with a complex genesis behind it. A similar shift of the poet's purpose also occurred at the hands of Edward Marsh, who requested that 'The Sentimental Exile' should be changed to 'The Old Vicarage, Grantchester'.

The war sonnets are poetry for the cenotaph and public parade. They appeal to mass comradeship, faith in a stern God as opposed to Brooke's own Apollonian and pagan leanings, 'our heritage', and the silence after battle. They are about abstract qualities, Love, Honour and Nobleness, conveniently omitting the process whereby the hopeful recruit materializes into the honoured dead. They are poems about self-destruction, how the 'I' becomes 'we' and eventually an 'it', a 'pulse in the eternal mind, no less'. War achieves this noble transformation; Menelaus no longer undertakes war for the object of winning Helen, but to give up his individuality and rid himself of personal 'evil'. The reader can spot Brooke in the midst of this public attitudinizing and recognize the ex-lover in search of a meaningful purpose. The problem here is that Brooke writes himself into a position of collusion with the dominant class of politicians and industrialists who supported the war effort, and whom he had derided in his Fabian and neo-pagan period. As a much-travelled socialist, he could have extended his patriotism to Commonwealth soldiers, the underclass, or the Europeans who suffered under war. But he does not do this, and by rewriting death as 'Peace', danger as 'Safety', and corpses as 'the rich dead', he unwittingly plays into the hands of the patriotic John Rumps – self-righteous, unquestioning and comfortable. It is the lack of questioning in the war sonnets which makes them so dangerous, and such fit material for ceremonies. Furthermore, in a national emergency, Brooke has been reclaimed by his class. He becomes the well-brought-up English gentleman, taking the playing fields of Rugby into the battlefields of France. Brooke's public front and private duplicity on this matter are demonstrated by the quotation at the head of this chapter, written in a letter of January 1915 to John Drinkwater. 'Come and die. It'll be great fun' is typical of the flippant, Janus-headed Brooke which the reader can recognize from the correspondence, a man full of questions and contradictions.

Rogers' *Reappraisal* volume reminds the reader that Brooke was not solely a poet, even though his huge sales after his death, and his posthumous reputation, have focused on his poetry. Brooke was stagestruck, and an avid theatregoer; his interests were wide, ranging from the newly imported 'ragtime' craze to the Russian ballet and Ibsen. He kept his theatre programmes, and students in the King's College archive can build up an accurate picture of his tastes and visits. It was only a matter of time before he would make his own serious attempt at dramatic writing. *Lithuania* (1912) is a bleak, expressionistic work, sharing in the Georgian realism that alarmed critics at the performances of *The End of the World* and *King Lear's Wife*. But Brooke's play has a borrowed plot, unfortunately one so hackneyed that several theatres approached by the author would not contemplate a performance of it. Miss A. E. F. Horniman, of the Manchester Repertory Theatre, complained in her rejection letter that it was the sixth play she had received on the same subject.

Lithuania takes place in a remote peasant hut, with an economy of casting and set. A stranger is lodging with a peasant family, who plot to kill him for his money once he is sleeping off his meal. The Father works up his courage by drinking in the nearby village, and in his absence, the loutish Daughter and her Mother do the killing of the stranger instead. He is later revealed as the returning son of the house, who disappeared twenty years previously to seek his fortune. The plot is pure melodrama, yet Brooke adopts a sparse style to emphasize the starkness and simplicity of the tragedy. This can render the play stilted in performance, but, in the hands of a skilled avant-garde director, it has dramatic momentum and power. Noticeably, Brooke has the ability to create suspense – the audience knows that a murdered man lies upstairs, unlike the befuddled drunken Father, who still thinks he has the job to do while realization dawns on the people around him. There is also black humour, when the Vodka Shop Keeper (who has returned to the hut with the Father) cannot understand the family's reactions:

MOTHER (*looking down the table*)   You knew him?
VODKA SHOP KEEPER (*blearily*)   Bless you, yes! – when he talked of old times. What are you all looking like that for? Didn't he come on here?
DAUGHTER He did.

(*Pause. Vodka Shop Keeper stares resentfully*)

VODKA SHOP KEEPER You're not very cheerful.

The potential for a laugh on this line is emphasized by the pause immediately before it. Brooke goes on to handle several strands of emotion in the climax of the play, and it closes on a scene of chaos. Characters are traumatized, shrieking, stumbling around inebriated, and backing off in horror. Yet Brooke creates this with a minimum number of words from the cast, leaving the situation to speak for itself. *Lithuania* is a small achievement, one which at least shows us Brooke's competence as a dramatic writer, if not great potential. Like so much of his output, it is a beginning.

Brooke's posthumous fame and his generous bequest to his Georgian friends meant that the future careers of Gibson, Abercrombie and Walter de la Mare were safeguarded from the worst that poverty could throw at them. His will had arranged that any royalties from his poetry sales should be divided equally between his colleagues, little realizing the enormous popularity his work would achieve. Thus, three Georgians were freed to write in a way that other poets were not, although only de la Mare achieved lasting popular success. In common with the other young writers who died in the 1914–18 conflict, it is impossible to say where Brooke's diverse talents would have led him. We presume, on the evidence of his two books, that he would have continued as a poet. Virginia Woolf, however, seems to have other ideas:

He was, I thought, the ablest of the young men; I didn't think much then of his poetry, which he read aloud on the lawn, but I thought he would be Prime Minister, because he had such a gift with people, and such sanity and force.... My idea was that he was to be a member of Parliament and edit the Classics, a very powerful, ambitious man, but not a poet. (*RB* 529)

Not a poet, not a playwright, but a politician. And, in providing a legacy for his Georgian colleagues, Brooke was putting his beliefs of state funding for the arts into practice.[7]

Afterword

> I found, ten years ago, that there were a number of writers doing work which appeared to me extremely good, but which was narrowly known; and I thought that anyone, however unprofessional and meagrely gifted, who presented a conspectus of it in a challenging and manageable form might be doing a good turn both to the poets and the reading public.

So wrote Edward Marsh in the valedictory preface to *Georgian Poetry 1920–22*, in 1922. The anthologies published by Marsh and Monro from the Poetry Bookshop survived one of the most traumatic periods of European history, and continued to promote Georgian work into the 1920s. However, competition provided by rival anthologies, notably *Poems of Today* (managed by Frank Sidgwick of Sidgwick & Jackson) meant that sales figures were undermined. The proliferation of anthologies by the end of the 1920s caused Robert Graves and Laura Riding to issue a pamphlet, *Against Anthologies* (1928), arguing that the anthology movement in general prevented the public from buying whole books by modern poets. The arts, too, had undergone a dramatic change during 1914–18, so that the initially scattered and eccentric-seeming 'isms' had gained a foothold with the reading public and (more noticeably) with the intellectuals who could further the alternative modernist cause. One of the most consistent driving forces in this direction was Richard Aldington (1892–1962), himself a poet, who had also gained his first publication at the hands of Harold Monro.

Furthermore, two of the most challenging and rigorous Georgians, Brooke and Thomas, were dead. Brooke's death alone caused the cessation of *New Numbers* in the spring of 1915. It had been a journal with a future and a mission, but quite simply the heart went out of the enterprise once Brooke's death was announced. Brooke lived on as a national icon, but it was another decade before Thomas's poetry began to occupy the position it has today. Frost, tangentially connected with the Georgian movement, returned to America in 1915; and Abercrombie, whose enthusiasm had been channelled into criticism, had given up his dream of being a poet in the country. Drinkwater had seceded even earlier, turning to the commercial drama circuit in preference to the art-dramas he had envisaged before 1917.

It is tempting to say that those who abandoned Georgianism early on stood the best chance of surviving in the post-1918 artistic climate. But, in many ways, the early Georgians *were* the modernists. Gibson, Brooke and Thomas were not anti-modern, or unmodern – they were the new poets, alongside *Des Imagistes* as anthologized by Ezra Pound. Pound wanted to wake up British art and 'make it new', unconcerned that this was also the aim of Edward Marsh and Harold Monro. Only the verse of Abercrombie and Drinkwater seems at odds with modernism as a whole, with Drinkwater too conventional in spirit for any rugged assault on the domain of poetic art, and Abercrombie's boundless inventiveness leading him backwards instead of forwards. The original concept of Georgianism did not mean rural verse, or anything remotely easy and sugared; as exemplified by Gibson, Thomas and Brooke, it can be contradictory, sharp and democratic. And it is the democratizing of poetry which is the greatest legacy of Marsh's experiment, with the new Georgian verse finding acceptance with the British public at a time when poetry was in the post-Aesthetic doldrums. In a century which has seen the marketing and presentation of poets as one facet of a cultural industry, the Georgians were the precursors of a trend.

Notes

INTRODUCTION

1. Edward ('Eddie') Marsh (1872–1953), private secretary to Winston Churchill and arts patron.
2. *The Letters of Rupert Brooke*, ed. Geoffrey Keynes (Faber & Faber, 1968), 597.
3. *A Boy's Will* was published by David Nutt, 1913.
4. John Freeman and Walter de la Mare offered to stand down, but Marsh and his publisher Monro had already decided against Thomas.
5. Abercrombie lived at The Gallows, Ryton, 2 miles from Dymock.
6. Oldfields is situated off an unclassified road, south of the A449 from Ledbury, on the Herefordshire border.
7. Situated at a crossroads approximately two miles north of Dymock on the Ledbury road.

CHAPTER 1.   LASCELLES ABERCROMBIE

1. *Gloucester Journal*, 12 January 1935.
2. Edward Marsh reported using the Abercrombie shower unit, made from a length of rubber tube attached to a cold-water pump (*EM* 242).
3. 1875–1947. Occultist and writer, sometime member of the Golden Dawn esoteric society alongside W. B. Yeats.
4. Brooke archive, L1, postcard dated 31 March 1913.
5. Thomas was initially enthusiastic about Abercrombie's work, but he developed doubts later on: letter to John Freeman, 8 March 1915.

CHAPTER 2. WILFRID GIBSON

1. *Hexham Courant*, 29 September 1978.
2. An American journal. This article, by the Reverend John Haynes Holmes, is titled 'Wilfred [sic] Wilson Gibson, Poet of Tenement and Trench.'
3. Correspondence between Gibson and Walter de la Mare is in the Bodleian Library, at de la Mare box number 26.
4. On being offered poor terms for a BBC reading, Auden declined to do it. The fee was doubled as a result. (Letter, 24 November 1937.)
5. *Gloucester Journal*, 15 December 1934.

CHAPTER 3. EDWARD THOMAS

1. The background to this comment from the late laureate Hughes is given in Sean Street's *The Dymock Poets* (Seren Borderlines, 1994), 155.
2. Ms.Eng.Lett.c.280. The Hootons (Harry and Janet) were old friends of the Thomases.
3. Harry Hooton, quoted in William Cooke's *Edward Thomas: A Critical Biography, 1878–1917* (Faber & Faber, 1970), 59.
4. *Daily News and Leader*, 22 July 1914.
5. Frost's disillusion with Gibson was not mutual. Gibson planned a successor to *New Numbers* in 1915, and wished to include Frost (letter to de la Mare, 10 August 1915).
6. Jeffrey Meyers, *Robert Frost: A Biography* (Constable, 1996), 122.
7. William Cooke, *Critical Biography*, 53.
8. Linda Hart, *Once They Lived in Gloucestershire: A Dymock Poets Anthology* (Lechlade: Green Branch Press, 1995), 81.
9. *The Collected Poems of Edward Thomas*, ed. R. George Thomas (Oxford University Press, 1978), p. 50, ll. 34–43.

CHAPTER 4. JOHN DRINKWATER

1. *Discovery: being the second book of an autobiography, 1897–1913* (Ernest Benn, 1932), 152. This account was preceded by *Inheritance: being the first book of an autobiography* (Ernest Benn, 1931). A third book did not occur.
2. *Discovery*, 149.
3. Composers, both connected with the Birmingham Midland Institute. Boughton (1878–1960) wrote the music for Drinkwater's

An English Medley, 1911. His operatic hit, *The Immortal Hour*, performed at the Repertory Theatre in 1921, starred Ffrancon-Davies.

4. Mary C. Sturgeon, *Studies of Contemporary Poets*, (Harrap, 1916). The book includes essays on Abercrombie, Brooke and Gibson.
5. *Discovery*, 155.
6. *Poems 1908–1914* (Sidgwick & Jackson, 1917), 97.
7. *Swords and Ploughshares* (Sidgwick & Jackson, 1915), 30.
8. *Poems 1908–1914*, 82.
9. Lascelles Abercrombie, 'The Drama of John Drinkwater', in *Four Decades of English Poetry 1890–1930*, vol. 1, no. 4 (July 1977), J. Cooper and E. Safer.
10. *Georgian Poetry 1916–17*, ed. Edward Marsh (Monro, Poetry Bookshop, 1917), 58.
11. *Abraham Lincoln* (Sidgwick & Jackson, 1918), 38–9. Single play editions have been used for this chapter, but readers may prefer the *Collected Plays* for convenience, as given in the Bibliography.
12. *Abraham Lincoln*, 27.
13. *Mary Stuart* (Sidgwick & Jackson, 1922), 55.
14. *Mary Stuart*, 26.
15. *Mary Stuart*, 76.
16. *Mary Stuart*, 18, 56 and 77.

CHAPTER 5.   RUPERT BROOKE

1. Brooke archive, L1, dated 18 November 1912.
2. 1892–1969. Her letters are published in *Song of Love: the letters of Rupert Brooke and Noel Olivier 1909–1915*, ed. Pippa Harris (Bloomsbury, 1991).
3. For a full-length study of literary estates and the problems of biography, see *Keepers of the Flame* by Ian Hamilton (Hutchinson 1992).
4. Timothy Rogers, *Rupert Brooke: A Reappraisal and Selection* (Routledge & Kegan Paul, 1971), 176–9.
5. See Browning's 'Home Thoughts from Abroad', with its 'first fine careless rapture'.
6. The numbered war sonnets were preceded by another, 'The Treasure', in their first appearance in *New Numbers*.
7. See his Fabian paper *Democracy and the Arts*, published in 1946.

Select Bibliography

ARCHIVE SOURCES

Birmingham Central Library. Newspaper reviews, playbills, Birmingham Repertory Theatre.

Birmingham University Archives. A Drinkwater collection; letters and editions.

Bodleian Library, Oxford. Manuscript poems and letters by Gibson, Drinkwater, Thomas.

Brotherton Library, Leeds University. Extensive collections of Abercrombie, Drinkwater, Gibson.

Dymock Poets Archive, Cheltenham & Gloucester College of Higher Education. Letter copies, Edward Thomas to Robert Frost, John Freeman and others. Reviews, photographs, and personal documents relating to the Dymock Poets. A wide selection of editions, journals, and critical works, including many listed under the following sections here. An *Occasional Papers* series, giving contemporary angles on the Dymock/Georgian Poets and their associates.

Gloucester City Libraries Local Studies Collection. Newspaper articles by J. W. Haines on Thomas, Frost, Gibson and Abercrombie. First editions by allied Glos. writers.

King's College Library, Cambridge. Brooke archive, poems and letters; related material.

COLLECTED EDITIONS

Brooke and Thomas are widely available in modern, cheap editions; Drinkwater and Gibson are out of print apart from a few anthologized poems. Abercrombie is out of print.

Abercrombie, Lascelles, *Interludes and Poems* (John Lane/The Bodley Head, 1928). A reprint of his 1908 collection.

Abercrombie, Lascelles, *The Poems of Lascelles Abercrombie* (Oxford University Press, 1930).

Brooke, Rupert, *The Works of Rupert Brooke* (Ware: Wordsworth Poetry Library, 1994).

_____ *The Poetical Works of Rupert Brooke*, ed. Geoffrey Keynes (Faber & Faber, 1946). A comprehensive edition compiled by Brooke's friend and literary executor.

Drinkwater, John, *Collected Plays*, vols. 1 and 2 (Sidgwick & Jackson, 1925). Includes his pageants written for the workforce at Cadbury's of Birmingham, as well as his early stage works.

_____ *Collected Poems*, vols. 1 and 2 (Sidgwick & Jackson, 1923 and 1925). His numerous books of early verse in two sets.

_____ *Discovery: being the second book of an autobiography, 1897–1913* (Ernest Benn, 1932). Early career, before his theatrical success. A surprisingly pedestrian account.

_____ *Prose Papers* (Elkin Mathews, 1917). Drinkwater the essayist and polemicist; includes two pieces on Brooke.

Gibson, Wilfrid Wilson, *Collected Poems 1905–1925* (Macmillan, 1926). Not a 'complete poems' but includes his Georgian era works.

_____ *Wilfrid Gibson* (Benn's Augustan series, 1931). A selection of 22 poems in a series which included major poets.

Hart, Linda (ed.) *Once They Lived in Gloucestershire: A Dymock Poets Anthology* (Lechlade: Green Branch Press, 1995). The Georgian/ Dymock group appear in the same anthology for the first time. Lively introductory essays on each poet.

Marsh, Edward (ed.), *Georgian Poetry 1911–12* (Monro, The Poetry Bookshop, 1912).

_____ *Georgian Poetry 1913–15* (Monro, the Poetry Bookshop, 1915).

_____ *Georgian Poetry 1916–17* (Monro, The Poetry Bookshop, 1917).

_____ *Georgian Poetry 1918–19* (Monro, The Poetry Bookshop, 1919).

_____ *Georgian Poetry 1920–22* (Monro, The Poetry Bookshop, 1922). These five anthologies were central to Georgianism as a literary movement, containing many poems by the 'Dymock' group.

New Numbers, vol. 1, nos. 1–4 (Dymock, Glos.: Ryton, 1914). The forum for the Dymock Poets. Rare; hard to obtain.

Thomas, Edward, *The Collected Poems of Edward Thomas*, ed. R. George Thomas (Oxford University Press, 1978). Good for editorial details..

_____ *Edward Thomas on the Countryside: A Selection of his Prose and Verse* (Faber & Faber, 1977). Thomas the countryman, with useful extracts from his numerous prose books.

_____ *The Works of Edward Thomas* (Ware: Wordsworth Poetry Library, 1994).

SECONDARY SOURCES AND CRITICAL STUDIES

Brooke, Frost and Thomas are well served by critical studies and biographical material. The works quoted here are a selection; the emphasis is on works produced after 1960.

Abercrombie, Lascelles, 'The Drama of John Drinkwater', in *Four Decades of Poetry 1890–1930*, vol. 1, no. 4 (July 1977), ed. Jeffrey Cooper and Esther Safer.

Clark, Keith, *The Muse Colony* (Bristol: Redcliffe Press, 1992). A similar approach to Street, but less comprehensive.

Cooke, William, *Edward Thomas: A Critical Biography, 1878–1917* (Faber & Faber, 1970). Packed with interesting quotations; clear and well written, and good for specialists and non-specialists alike.

Delaney, Paul, *The Neo-Pagans: Friendship and Love in the Rupert Brooke Circle* (Macmillan, 1987). An entertaining study, reorienting Brooke in his original socio-political context.

Elton, Oliver, *Lascelles Abercrombie 1881–1938*, British Academy booklets, vol. xxv (Humphrey Milford, no date).

Farjeon, Eleanor, *Edward Thomas: The Last Four Years* (Oxford University Press, 1978). An account from a friend who knew the poet and his family.

Harvey, Anne (ed.), *Elected Friends: Poems for and about Edward Thomas* (Enitharmon Press, 1991). Shows the impact of Thomas on later generations of poets.

Hassall, Christopher, *Edward Marsh: Patron of the Arts: A Biography* (Longmans, 1959). Exemplary detailed scholarship; good for historical background.

——*Rupert Brooke: A Biography* (Faber & Faber, 1964). A standard biography.

Hogg, Roger, 'W. W. Gibson: The People's Poet', *Occasional Papers Series*, no. 2, ed. Dr Peter Easy (Cheltenham & Gloucester College of Higher Education, 1996).

Keynes, Geoffrey (ed.), *Rupert Brooke, Collected Letters* (Faber & Faber, 1968). Indicative of the 'real' Brooke.

Marsh, Jan, 'Georgian Poetry and the Land' (PhD thesis, Sussex University, 1973). A well-researched study.

Meyers, Jeffrey, *Robert Frost: A Biography* (Constable, 1996). A concise biography of an important Georgian associate.

Rogers, Timothy (ed.), *Georgian Poetry 1911–1922: The Critical Heritage* (Routledge & Kegan Paul, 1977). A selection of reviews and critical writings dating from the appearance of the first Georgian anthology, with an overview and brief biographical details.

—— *Rupert Brooke: A Reappraisal and Selection* (Routledge & Kegan Paul, 1971). Lesser-known Brooke works in one convenient volume.

Ross, Robert H., *The Georgian Revolt: Rise and Fall of a Poetic Ideal, 1910–22* (Faber & Faber, 1967). Valuable historical account, more wide-ranging and academic than Street and Clark.

Smith, Stan, *Edward Thomas*, Faber Student Guides (Faber & Faber, 1986). Thomas and engagement with society; a socialist interpretation of the poetry and prose.

Street, Sean, *The Dymock Poets* (Bridgend: Seren Borderlines, 1994). A traditional literary/historical study; much information about the poets and their lives during 1914.

Thomas, Helen, and Myfanwy Thomas, *Under Storm's Wing* (Paladin/ Carcanet, 1990). A moving account of the Thomas family, useful for gender issues and social context.

Thomas, R. George, *Edward Thomas: A Portrait* (Clarendon, 1985). A compact biography with plenty of quotation from sources.

Index

*Recent and
Forthcoming Titles
in the
New Series of*

WRITERS AND
THEIR WORK

"... *this series promises to outshine its own
previously high reputation.*"
Times Higher Education Supplement

"...*will build into a fine multi-volume critical
encyclopaedia of English literature.*"
Library Review & Reference Review

"...*Excellent, informative, readable, and recommended.*"
NATE News

"*written by outstanding contemporary critics,
whose expertise is flavoured by unashamed enthusiasm for
their subjects and the series' diverse aspirations.*"
Times Educational Supplement

"*A useful and timely addition to the ranks of the lit crit and
reviews genre. Written in an accessible and authoritative style.*"
Library Association Record

WRITERS AND THEIR WORK
RECENT & FORTHCOMING TITLES

Title	Author
Peter Ackroyd	*Susana Onega*
Kingsley Amis	*Richard Bradford*
Anglo-Saxon Verse	*Graham Holderness*
Antony and Cleopatra	*Ken Parker*
As You Like It	*Penny Gay*
W.H. Auden	*Stan Smith*
Alan Ayckbourn	*Michael Holt*
J.G. Ballard	*Michel Delville*
Aphra Behn	*Sue Wiseman*
John Betjeman	*Dennis Brown*
Edward Bond	*Michael Mangan*
Anne Brontë	*Betty Jay*
Emily Brontë	*Stevie Davies*
A.S. Byatt	*Richard Todd*
Caroline Drama	*Julie Sanders*
Angela Carter	*Lorna Sage*
Geoffrey Chaucer	*Steve Ellis*
Children's Literature	*Kimberley Reynolds*
Caryl Churchill	*Elaine Aston*
John Clare	*John Lucas*
S.T. Coleridge	*Stephen Bygrave*
Joseph Conrad	*Cedric Watts*
Crime Fiction	*Martin Priestman*
John Donne	*Stevie Davies*
Carol Ann Duffy	*Deryn Rees Jones*
George Eliot	*Josephine McDonagh*
English Translators of Homer	*Simeon Underwood*
Henry Fielding	*Jenny Uglow*
E.M. Forster	*Nicholas Royle*
Elizabeth Gaskell	*Kate Flint*
The Georgian Poets	*Rennie Parker*
William Golding	*Kevin McCarron*
Graham Greene	*Peter Mudford*
Hamlet	*Ann Thompson & Neil Taylor*
Thomas Hardy	*Peter Widdowson*
David Hare	*Jeremy Ridgman*
Tony Harrison	*Joe Kelleher*
William Hazlitt	*J. B. Priestley; R. L. Brett (intro. by Michael Foot)*
Seamus Heaney	*Andrew Murphy*
George Herbert	*T.S. Eliot (intro. by Peter Porter)*
Henrik Ibsen	*Sally Ledger*
Henry James – The Later Writing	*Barbara Hardy*
James Joyce	*Steven Connor*
Julius Caesar	*Mary Hamer*
Franz Kafka	*Michael Wood*
William Langland: *Piers Plowman*	*Claire Marshall*
King Lear	*Terence Hawkes*
Philip Larkin	*Laurence Lerner*
D.H. Lawrence	*Linda Ruth Williams*
Doris Lessing	*Elizabeth Maslen*
C.S. Lewis	*William Gray*
David Lodge	*Bernard Bergonzi*
Christopher Marlowe	*Thomas Healy*
Andrew Marvell	*Annabel Patterson*
Ian McEwan	*Kiernan Ryan*
Measure for Measure	*Kate Chedgzoy*
A Midsummer Night's Dream	*Helen Hackett*

RECENT & FORTHCOMING TITLES

Title	Author
Vladimir Nabokov	*Neil Cornwell*
V. S. Naipaul	*Suman Gupta*
Walter Pater	*Laurel Brake*
Brian Patten	*Linda Cookson*
Sylvia Plath	*Elisabeth Bronfen*
Jean Rhys	*Helen Carr*
Richard II	*Margaret Healy*
Dorothy Richardson	*Carol Watts*
John Wilmot, Earl of Rochester	*Germaine Greer*
Romeo and Juliet	*Sasha Roberts*
Christina Rossetti	*Kathryn Burlinson*
Salman Rushdie	*Damian Grant*
Paul Scott	*Jacqueline Banerjee*
The Sensation Novel	*Lyn Pykett*
P.B. Shelley	*Paul Hamilton*
Wole Soyinka	*Mpalive Msiska*
Edmund Spenser	*Colin Burrow*
J.R.R. Tolkien	*Charles Moseley*
Leo Tolstoy	*John Bayley*
Charles Tomlinson	*Tim Clark*
Anthony Trollope	*Andrew Sanders*
Victorian Quest Romance	*Robert Fraser*
Angus Wilson	*Peter Conradi*
Mary Wollstonecraft	*Jane Moore*
Virginia Woolf	*Laura Marcus*
Working Class Fiction	*Ian Haywood*
W.B. Yeats	*Edward Larrissy*
Charlotte Yonge	*Alethea Hayter*

TITLES IN PREPARATION

UPPINGHAM SCHOOL LIBRARY

R44483K2758